CONTENT CRITIC

CONTENT CRITICAL

Gaining Competitive Advantage
Through High-Quality Web Content

GERRY MCGOVERN

ROB NORTON

FINANCIAL TIMES
Prentice Hall

PEARSON EDUCATION LIMITED

Head Office:
Edinburgh Gate
Harlow CM20 2JE
Tel: +44 (0)1279 623623
Fax: +44 (0)1279 431059

London Office:
128 Long Acre
London WC2E 9AN
Tel: +44 (0)20 7447 2000
Fax: +44 (0)20 7240 5771
Website: www.business-minds.com

First published in Great Britain in 2002

© Pearson Education Limited 2002

The right of Gerry McGovern and Rob Norton to be identified as authors of this work has been asserted by them in accordance with the Copyright, Designs and Patents Act 1988.

ISBN: 0 273 65604 X

British Library Cataloguing in Publication Data
A CIP catalogue record for this book can be obtained from the British Library.

10 9 8 7 6 5 4 3 2 1

Typeset by Pantek Arts Ltd, Maidstone, Kent.
Printed and bound in Great Britain by Biddles Ltd, Guildford and King's Lynn

The Publishers' policy is to use paper manufactured from sustainable forests.

ACKNOWLEDGEMENTS

Screenshots on pages 50, 165 reprinted by permission from Cisco Systems. Screenshots on pages 52, 150, 191 reprinted by permission from Microsoft Corporation. Screenshot on page 56 reprinted by permission from Oracle Corporation. Screenshots on pages 91, 148, 163, 167 reprinted by permission from Cable News Network (CNN) LP, LLLP. Screenshots on pages 138, 147 reprinted by permission from Dell Computer Corporation. Screenshot on page 139 reprinted by permission from Google Inc. Screenshots on pages 148, 163 reprinted by permission from International Business Machines Corporation. Screenshots on pages 150, 160, 161, 166 reprinted by permission from Yahoo! Inc. Screenshots on pages 151, 167 reprinted by permission from Iomega Corporation. Screenshot on page 162 reprinted by permission from Amazon.com. Screenshot on page 166 reprinted by permission from E*TRADE Group, Inc.

CONTENTS

EVERYTHING YOU KNOW ABOUT PUBLISHING IS WRONG

1

"The Internet will make every enterprise a publisher."

Steve Case, chairman and CEO of America Online, 2000

"The difficulty seems to be, not so much that we publish unduly in view of the extent and variety of present-day interests, but rather that publication has been extended far beyond our present ability to make real use of the record. The summation of human experience is being expanded at a prodigious rate, and the means we use for threading through the consequent maze to the momentarily important item is the same as was used in the days of square-rigged ships."

Vannevar Bush, "As we may think," Atlantic Monthly, 1945

"The concept of the Web is of universal readership. If you publish a document on the Web, it is important that anyone who has access to it can read it and link to it."

Tim Berners-Lee, inventor of the World Wide Web, 1991

You want to know the secret of a successful website? You want to know the Holy Grail of the Web? Sure you do. That's why you picked up this book.

There are two facts about the Web that are vastly under-appreciated. The first is that the primary thing people do on the Web is read. That's why this book calls people who visit your website "readers" instead of that ugly, generic, drug-associated, catch-all, mean-nothing term, "user."

The second fact is that readers come to the Web to *gather* content. Think about it for a moment. Readers come to the Web to gather or review content, rather than specifically to search or find content. The difference is subtle, but it's critical.

It's like this. Most of the time the reader (customer, staff, supplier, investor) doesn't know exactly what content they are looking for. They're interested in a particular subject area, product type, or other general area of interest. Only in a minority of cases does the reader know precisely what content they want.

The traditional approach of data/content management deals reasonably well with readers who know the exact name of the document they are looking for. But it deals very poorly with readers who have a general idea of what they want. In other words, the approach to dealing with content that most organizations take today fails most of its readers most of the time. The result we see everywhere. It's called information overload.

What's the solution? What's the secret that will make your website succeed where so many others fail? The secret can be summarized in one word:

PUBLISHING

The Web is a medium for publishing content. What? Surely publishing is about Harry Potter and *The Wall Street Journal*. It's about James Joyce and *Sports Illustrated*. Wrong. If part of your job involves writing original content, whether that be a technical paper for a product, or a marketing pitch for that product, you're part of a publishing process. If you find that you're spending more and more time reading stuff in order to help you do your job better, you're directly affected by publishing. The modern world runs on content. We're either publishers or consumers of it. Mostly, we're both.

If you work for an organization, and part of your job is to write for that organization, you should read this book. If part of your job is to edit the written work of others and then publish that work on an intranet or internet website, then you should read this book. If your job is to help your organization create, edit and publish content more efficiently, then you should read this book. If you do any of the above, then whether you know it or not, you're involved in publishing.

Content is written-down intellectual capital. It is the lifeblood of the information organization, and the publishing processes and systems are its heart and arteries. The organization that doesn't understand how to publish content professionally will play a diminishing role in an increasingly information-driven economy. In a world dominated by information, publishing skills are no longer something that's nice to have. They are a must-have.

As a recent A.T. Kearney study put it, "digital content is becoming key to a company's ability to develop and expand commerce, foster collaboration within and between organizations, personalize sales and customer service, and disseminate information both internally and externally." Content is critical.

IT'S AN INFORMATION OVERLOADED WORLD

Welcome to information overload. Get used to it, because it's going to get a lot worse. In an industrial economy we face issues of scarcity. Oil is scarce, prices go up. In a digital economy, we face issues of glut. Things digital have a close-to-zero cost to reproduce, therefore they are endlessly reproduced.

Consider the following:

- Every issue of *The New York Times* contains more information than someone in the 17th century would have read in a lifetime.
- There is enough scientific information written every year to keep a person busy reading day and night for 460 years.

- In the past 30 years we have produced more information than in the previous 5,000.
- The amount of recorded scientific knowledge is doubling approximately every 15 to 20 years.
- More than 1,000 books are published around the world every day.
- Every day seven million new documents are published on the Web, where there are already more than 550 billion.
- The world produces between one and two exabytes of unique content per year, which is roughly 250 megabytes for every man, woman and child on earth.

The Web is the Trojan Horse of information overload. It promised information nirvana and delivered overload hell. Someone once said that searching for information on the Web was like drinking water from a fire hose. Not surprisingly a 2000 survey by Roper Starch Worldwide found that 71 percent of people using the Internet become frustrated when searching.

TRADITIONAL PUBLISHING SUCKS

Walk into a newsagent and be stunned by the amount of magazines and newspapers on offer. There used to be an ad for a "serious" newspaper that said: miss reading this paper and you miss an important part of the day. The joke went around that if you fully read the paper you would miss the *entire* day. Walk into a bookstore and be overawed by the massive selection of books available. Remember, even the biggest bookstore in the world can display only a tiny fraction of the books currently in print.

Traditional publishing sucks. Publishing is the art and science of moving content from the creator (author) to the consumer (reader). But it doesn't work very well. It's haphazard, slow, and wildly inefficient. Who are the publishers and editors who decide what gets published when? What do they know? Aren't they overpaid middlemen who always miss the really good stuff? Why should we trust their judgment? Why should we wait for their opinion on what we should and shouldn't read?

If you read two books every week, you would be reading only three ten-thousandths of what's published. And even if you had time to read more books, how would you even find out which were worth reading?

And why is it that so many books and magazines are published? Think of the 1,000-plus books published around the world every day. Can you believe that? If you read two books every week, you would be reading only three ten-thousandths of what's published. And even if you had time to read more books, how would you even find out which were worth reading? In the US alone, nearly 5,000 different magazines are published. Of all copies printed, more than half are returned to the publishers unsold.

Meanwhile, the whole publishing industry charges too much for its services. Libraries around the world, particularly those attached to universities, are in crisis. Prices for academic journals have spiraled out of control. The very content that is the fuel that universities run on is simply getting too expensive.

There has to be an alternative, right?

THE ALTERNATIVE SUCKS 30,000 TIMES MORE

The alternative is 30,000 times more frightening. So, you think there are too many magazines, newspapers and books in print? Consider this carefully. According to a 2000 study by the University of California, Berkeley, printed content represents 0.003 percent of all content published annually around the world. That statistic is worth repeating:

Printed content represents 0.003 percent of all content published annually around the world.

Think about all those bookstores. Think about all those books, magazines and newspapers. All that massive, massive quantity of print still only represents 0.003 percent of total content.

Where is all the rest of it published? The vast majority of content in the world can be found on computer disks. In comparison with computers print publishing is a miser. Print is simply not at the races. You see, the real problem we face today is not what is being published in print, it's what is being "published" to disk.

For every sentence published in print there are 30,000 sentences published on computers. For every book printed there are some 30,000 "books" published on computers. Traditional publishing may not be working when it comes to print, but at least it has made some effort to keep the floodgates shut. That's because the average publisher will reject up to 90 percent of publishing proposals they get.

In the world of computers the floodgates have been blown from their hinges. Information has gone haywire on computers because there are little or no publishing standards. Everyone is a publisher, most of it is awful, and nobody has time to read anywhere remotely near what's out there. Even if they want to read a specific document, there's so much content, so badly organized, that the effort in finding it is often not worth the trouble. As Neil Postman puts it, "We have transformed information into a form of garbage."

Yet people are reading more because they have to. People are writing more because they have to. Content is critical to the success of the modern organization and individual. Publishing may suck, but its alternative is far, far worse. No matter what way you slice it, getting better at publishing is the only way you're going to get better at content.

The essence of publishing is communication. The essence of great publishing is about getting the right content to the right person at the right time – and making a profit out of it. Increasingly, that's what modern business is about, whether that content is going to a member of corporate staff, a supplier, a customer or investor, and whether that content is helping to sell a product or support it.

ORGANIZATIONS ARE AWFUL AT PUBLISHING CONTENT

Imagine for a moment the modern factory floor. Everything is clean and tidy. The machines are well organized. The processes work with great precision. Efficiency and productivity are maximized. A good manager will not allow a thing to get out of place.

Try to imagine what the contents of your computer or website would look like if they were presented like a factory floor. If they are like a great many other websites, they'd look less like a factory floor and more like a local dump – an information dump.

A modern manager would never let their factory floor get in the state they let their websites get into. One reason is that you cannot *see* the state content is in. Another is that few people realize the true value or cost of content. Studies have shown that a quality document can cost $4,000 to get ready for publication. Think about it. That report on your desk probably cost more than the computer sitting beside it.

A great many managers think about content as being "stored" rather than "published" on computers. "The old dynamic of computing belongs to the golden age of information," Richard Hackathorn wrote in Byte Magazine in 1997. "It was the classical 'Request and Reply' (R&R) model." This indeed is the classic approach to information. The computer stores the content, and then the reader requests a specific document.

This model worked okay when there was a reasonable quantity of content and when the person knew exactly what they were looking for. The problem is that the amount of content has ballooned and that in the great majority of cases the reader often isn't quite sure exactly what they want. Therefore, the old model of how we deal with content on computers is not working. Organizations need a totally new approach; a publishing approach.

The Web is not the lost city of the geeks. It is not there so that the techies can take over the world. The Web is not "cutting edge" technology, but rather primitive technology. There is no such thing as a "webmaster." An Internet month is not like a normal year, because while there are now far more websites and people reading them, the underlying structures of the Web have not really changed in the past five years. Broadband is not a reality for the average consumer. Interactive TV is still a pipe dream. Virtual reality is still science fiction.

The Internet was invented as a communications medium and the Web was invented as a publishing solution for content. As *Publish* magazine stated in October 2000, "We stand on the threshold of a revolution. The increasing demand for businesses to reach the customer and each other has brought the world to another upheaval – an internet communication revolution."

"Strip away the highfalutin' talk, and at bottom, the Internet is a tool that dramatically lowers the cost of communication," *Business Week* wrote in March 2001. When America Online chairman Steve Case talked at the JP Morgan annual technology conference in May 2001, he stated that "the key driver" over the coming decade would be products and services "that really do give consumers better ways to get information or to communicate or to be entertained."

So, in essence, the Web is fundamentally a place where people come to publish and find content. The primary activity that a person does on a website is read. What's more, the Web is going to remain a publishing medium for text-based content (with simple graphics) for the next 20 years at least. Broadband, streaming video, virtual reality data suits, you name it, in time will all find a place in the great big Web. But in 2020, millions upon millions of people will still have everyday needs to read up on something, to learn more about something so that they can buy it, sell it or make it.

Tim Berners-Lee invented the World Wide Web because he realized that the traditional tools of publishing were not working. In the late Eighties there was a problem at the CERN Research Institute in Switzerland, where he worked. It was a classic problem of the new economy – getting the right information to the right people at the right time.

At CERN this problem was being addressed by the classic human network approach. If you wanted something you talked to somebody else in a corridor, in a canteen, on the phone, by email. That person scratched their head and said, maybe John knows where that research paper is, or maybe Mary has it on her computer, or give me a call later and I'll have a root around in my office, or did you check the filing cabinet in office 5A?

This classic approach worked very well in a situation where everybody knew everybody else, where things changed at a sensible pace, and where there was a reasonable quantity of content being created. It did not work in a new economy whose principal characteristics were the speed of change and the massive increase in the amount of content being created.

As a research institute, with lots of visiting researchers, CERN faced another key problem – a high turnover of people. "When two years is a typical length of stay, information is constantly being lost," Berners-Lee pointed out in his original proposal for the Web in 1990. "If a CERN experiment were a static once-only development, all the information could be written in a big book. As it is, CERN is constantly changing as new ideas are produced, as new technology becomes available, and in order to get around unforeseen technical problems … Keeping a book up to date becomes impractical, and the structure of the book needs to be constantly revised."

Does this sound like a problem your organization is facing today? Join the party! In 1990, Tim Berners-Lee had the vision to foresee that, "The problems of information loss may be particularly acute at CERN, but in this case (as in certain others), CERN is a model in miniature of the rest of the world in a few years' time. CERN meets now some problems which the rest of the world will have to face soon."

Technologists dreamed of the Web as automation heaven. Buy some software, get a website, and – presto – you were slashing costs and driving profits. It doesn't work that way. *People* communicate, *not* machines. *People* write content, *not* machines. Sure, software can make communication and publishing processes more efficient, but if the quality of communication and content isn't high to begin with, it's the classic "garbage in, garbage out" situation.

Business-to-business (B2B) commerce on the Web was seen as a radical development that would create the perfect "frictionless" marketplace. As more and more B2B websites bomb, a new reality is dawning. "Indeed, as many businesses now realize, the real gains from online B2B commerce will come not from trading but from better access to and the sharing of information," the McKinsey Quarterly stated in March 2001. "This information might include supply-and-demand forecasts, reports of inventory levels at points along the supply chain, and market-tested predictions of the effect that the price of futures and other options will have on the availability of particular supplies, such as electricity and paper."

Technology can make the communication more efficient, but technology can never write that easy-to-understand sales pitch for a product, never write that simple-to-follow installation guide for a piece of software.

The Internet and the Web bring together people who *have* content with people who *want* content. The Web allows organizations and individuals to receive and communicate information. Technology can make the communication more efficient, but technology can never write that easy-to-understand sales pitch for a product, never write that simple-to-follow installation guide for a piece of software, never write that exciting job description that makes someone want to join an organization. Technology can send an email auto-response, but technology can never write a personal reply that really answers the question and helps close the sale. Only people – people who know their stuff and know how to write well – can do that.

Let nobody tell you that the Internet was ever anything other than a communications medium. People like J.C.R. Licklider, who dreamed up the Internet in the sixties, had a vision. "We believe that we are entering a technological age," Licklider wrote, "in which we will be able to interact with the richness of living information – not merely in the passive way that we have become accustomed to using books and libraries, but as active participants in an ongoing process, bringing something to it through our interaction with it, and not simply receiving something from it by our connection to it."

Just what is publishing? Publishing means "to make public." It's all about taking an idea, polishing it up and sending it out to a group of readers. Publishers make money by turning ideas into valuable content. In this new economy we are all publishers. Publishing supports the sale of our products and services. It tells people why they should buy something, how they get it to work, and how to fix it when it goes wrong.

The majority of us already participate in at least some sort of publishing process. If we work with content that is intended to reach a readership, whether that be our managers, colleagues, customers or investors, we are already participating in a publishing process.

Here are a few fundamentals of publishing that are relevant to everyone involved in creating content:

- Publishing is about quality control. You will reject far more than you will publish. At the American Economic Review, for example, about 12 percent of the submitted articles are accepted.

- In publishing, less is invariably more. Critical content is precise and to the point. In this information overloaded world there has never been a greater need to keep it short, simple and snappy.

- The reader is king. If nobody reads you you're dead. Publishers who don't truly understand their readers – and publish content for those readers – go out of business.

- "Time-to-publish" is critical. It's not enough to have great content if you don't get it to your reader before your competitor does.

- Publishing is the business of profiting from content. A viable publisher knows how to make money – either directly or indirectly – out of content.

Today we are working with content more than we have ever done before. Tomorrow, and for the rest of our careers, publishing will become key to our success. Understanding and gaining the skills of publishing will help us progress. Failing to do so will limit our progress.

The key difference between commerce and e-commerce is that commerce is selling with people and e-commerce is selling with content. You buy from a website because it has content that answers questions about product range, features, availability, price, support, customer references, company background, etc. A publishing strategy delivers such content.

Those organizations which have made the Internet work have all embodied publishing principles in their approach. That goes for AOL Time Warner, Microsoft, Yahoo, Amazon and Cisco. In fact, there is hardly a successful website that does not embody a professional publishing approach. All great websites are fueled by great content.

Just what is content? And how does content relate to information and knowledge?

- Knowledge is the useful stuff that's inside our heads. It's our ideas, our experience, it's what we know about how things work, about how to make things better. We read content to gain knowledge.

- Information is the communication of knowledge. Information is a process, an activity. To inform is to impart knowledge to someone else. "10 percent off all TVs if you buy now!" is information at the point at which it is communicated. Information can be communicated in two ways. The first is informally, verbally. I meet you and I inform you, "Do you know there's a shop down the road and it has 10 percent off all TVs if you buy now?" The second way is to formally communicate information through content.

- Content is how we formally structure our knowledge. We do this by putting it on paper, by putting it on film, by putting it on tape, by putting it on the Web. The Web is a giant container for content! It has become the ultimate place we go to get content. The type of content that this book deals with is the content you read, because that represents the vast majority of content on the Web.

TIME-TO-PUBLISH

It used to be that within the organization information was like gold. It was hoarded (and still is!). It represented power and influence. If you wanted it you had to make a major effort to get it. But that entire dynamic has changed, driven by an information-hungry society and powered by the Internet.

Information has become like milk. You need to distribute it quickly or it becomes worthless. What you know right now is not nearly as important as your ability to learn more. Your ability to communicate what you know is as important as what you know. In an age of stability, those who *know* inherit the earth. In an age of change, those who know *how to know* inherit it!

We have come across the websites of major financial institutions which publish their Tuesday morning notes on the Web on a Friday. It is not uncommon to read about a major development in the papers, and to go to that organization's website and find nothing on it.

A defining characteristic of business over the past 30 years has been the focus on reducing the time-to-market for a product or service. In 1970, for example, it took 10 years to develop a new car. By 2000, it took less than five. If a computer printer develops a fault, the quicker content is placed on a website describing how to fix that fault the better. Publishing that content six weeks after that fault has been isolated is a lot less valuable than publishing it immediately.

A primary reason the Internet was invented was to get quality content published faster. "The importance of improving decision-making processes," J.C.R. Licklider and Robert Taylor wrote in 1968, "not only in government, but throughout business and the professions, is so great as to warrant every effort." Those organizations who will succeed in the future will be those who can get the right content to the right person before their competitor does.

Global Sources, a company that publishes business-to-business content that helps Asian producers sell internationally, has found that the Web greatly reduces time-to-publish. According to Andrew Tanzer, writing for *Forbes*, it can take more than two months for a print advertisement produced in Chengdu, the capital of Sichuan province, to reach an importer in New York. Today, Global Sources, using staff armed with digital cameras, laptops and modems, can have product information in front of a potential buyer within two hours instead of two months.

FIGURE 1.1

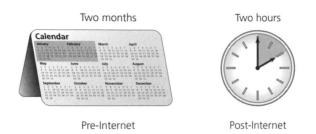

The Web has significantly reduced time-to-publish within the academic world. Taubes (1996) found that with appropriate content management systems in place, the time it takes an article to get published could be reduced by about two-thirds. While the Web gives the potential to publish faster, the reality for many websites is very different. We have come across the websites of major financial institutions which publish their Tuesday morning notes on the Web on a Friday. It is not uncommon to read about a major development in the papers, and to go to that organization's website and find nothing on it.

What this means is that, just because the Web allows you to publish faster, doesn't mean you will. Unless you have the appropriate commitment to the Web as a proper publishing medium, and unless you implement proper web publishing systems and processes, your content is likely to be published faster by print than online, even though the latter offers a faster time-to-publish potential.

THE ORGANIZATION AS UNIVERSITY

"The workplace is becoming more like a university setting," Duncan Campbell, an International Labor Organization economist, told *Newsweek* in 2001. Why? Well, you've heard the phrase "life-long learning." Life-long learning describes a world where we are constantly learning new things so as to be able to do our jobs. We don't just go to the university for four years now, but rather the university comes to us everyday of our lives.

Consider the following:

- A 1998 study by George Mason University of college graduates found that 95 percent of respondents view lifelong learning as an essential part of their career.
- According to a 2000 OECD report, since 1985 the expansion of knowledge-based industries has outpaced gross domestic product (GDP) growth in the developed countries. Knowledge-based industries now account for more than half of OECD-wide GDP.
- A 2000 PricewaterhouseCoopers report found that intellectual assets now account for 78 percent of the total value of American S&P 500 companies.

We are life-long learners in a quest to make ourselves more productive, more intelligent, more employable, more valuable. The organization is an information organization now. The organization is a university now. It must use information to make itself more productive, more innovative, more profitable, more competitive.

Academics were the original information workers. Universities were the original information organizations. The modern organization and individual can learn much with regard to becoming a better "information organization" by observing how academics and universities have dealt with content. Sure, they have made mistakes, but they have learned valuable lessons. Lessons we can all learn from.

The university is the home of the Internet. The Internet was invented by the US military in conjunction with several universities. The Internet was first embraced by universities. The Web was invented in a research organization. The Web was first embraced by universities. Do you see a pattern emerging?

The Internet and Web were embraced by universities around the world because academics and students saw in them tools for the better communication of ideas. These new tools were better than the older tools: letters, faxes, phones. The Internet and email allowed ideas to be shared more quickly, found more quickly, organized and published in a more efficient manner.

Content is the fuel that drives universities and academia. Such institutions have had to deal with the critical problem of maximizing the value they create from knowledge for centuries. They have found that one of the best ways to maximize the value of knowledge is to get it down on paper. They have found that one of the best ways to judge information workers (academics, scientists) is by what they publish.

Whether as creators of content, or through their libraries as organizers of content, academia has had to address how best to derive value from content; how best to get the right content to the right people at the right time. The academic organization has found that an essential way to derive value from knowledge is to get it published.

In fact, knowledge that is published is at the heart of the academic organization. Tenopir and King (1998) found that scientists view formal publication as either the most important or second most important source of knowledge, as compared with other sources, such as laboratory-instrument readouts, computer-based research, or advice from colleagues, library staff, and support staff.

What are the characteristics of the modern academic information organization and worker?

- They publish more than ever. About 4,000 academic papers are published every day in the US alone.

- They read more than ever. Between 1990 and 1993, for example, scientists at the University of Tennessee read an average of 188 scholarly articles per year.

- They communicate more than ever. *The Journal of Electronic Publishing* in 2000 reported on a study that found that scientists spend 50–60 percent of their time communicating.

"Publish or perish" has long been a motto for those who work in academia. Today, it becomes a motto for all information workers. Academics are the original "information workers." A large part of what they do is to come up with or explore ideas. They then publish the results as content, whether that be in the form of research papers, reports, studies, books, etc. If they don't publish, they don't get recognized by their peers and superiors, they don't get funding for further research, and their careers grind to a halt.

Resh (1998) states that, "Research articles... are the traditional 'coin of the realm' for academic scientists. Through their publications, scientists either become known or remain unknown. Moreover, their initial appointment and eventual tenure, promotions, and research funding are largely based on the quality and the quantity of their publications." According to Varian (1997), "At most academic organizations there is almost a frantic drive to publish. It can be dog-eat-dog, publish or perish. If you don't publish, you're not visible. If you're not visible, your career goes in reverse."

KNOW YOUR READER

Think of your website as a publication and it all begins to make a lot of sense. Think of the person who visits your website as a reader and your objectives become clearer. Because the Web is not all that different from all those other communication tools – print, phone, fax.

Yes, there are differences. Yes, Web publishing has different dynamics and rules from, say, print publishing. But the core objective is still the same – to communicate with other people.

The language that is used today to describe the Internet is dry, technical and non-descriptive. As someone pointed out, the only two groups of people who are called "users" are drug-users and computer-users. ("Traffic" is another word both have in common.) "User" is such an all-embracing word that it is essentially meaningless. "Usability" is a clunky, awkward word that lacks style and elegance. In this sense, it describes the opposite of what it's supposed to describe.

For centuries humans have described their tools and the people who use them by their primary function. We don't call people horse-users, car-users or pen-users. We call them riders, drivers and writers. We call a person who uses a bike a cyclist because cycling is the primary thing they do when using a bike. That doesn't stop them also being a saddle-sitter and handlebar-holder. We still call a computer a "computer" even though it does a lot more than compute.

The fact that we have not described the Web and the people who use it by their primary function has led to great confusion. *Content Critical* is about clearing up that confusion. It's about giving you a clear picture in language you can understand and relate to. *Content Critical* talks about a website as a publication, because that is the primary function of a website.

Yes, it's a different kind of publication. It's more interactive and transaction-driven than traditional publications, but it's still a publication. Like all publications it's a place where people come to be informed.

Content Critical looks on the person who visits your website as a reader. (If the primary activity of your website is audio or video, then you have listeners and viewers.) Here we should understand the larger meaning of "to read." To read is not simply to "interpret written symbols." The core root of "to read" is to "discern the meaning of something." That's what information workers do. The Web reader is highly educated, task-oriented and time-starved. They come to your website with the objective of finding stuff that will make them more knowledgeable; that will allow them to act. How you meet that objective is how they will judge you.

References

Tim Berners-Lee, "Information Management: A Proposal" (this is the original proposal for the World Wide Web). CERN, March 1989. http://www.w3. org History/1989/proposal.html

Tim Berners-Lee, "The World Wide Web – past, present and future," British Computer Society, July 1996. http://www.bcs.org.uk/news/ timbl.htm

Bo-Christer Björk and Ziga Turk, "How Scientists Retrieve Publications: An Empirical Study of How The Internet Is Overtaking Paper Media," *The Journal of Electronic Publishing*, December 2000, Volume 6, Issue 2

Vannevar Bush, "As We May Think," *The Atlantic Monthly*, July 1945 http://www.isg.sfu.ca/~duchier/misc/vbush/vbush-all.shtml

A.T. Kearney, *Network Publishing: Creating value through digital content*, April 2001 http://www.atkearney.com/main.taf?site=1&a=1&b= 5&c=1&d=75

J.C.R. Licklider, "Man-Computer Symbiosis," *IRE Transactions on Human Factors in Electronics*, Volume HFE-1, March 1960

J.C.R. Licklider and Robert Taylor, "The Computer as a Communication Device," *Science and Technology*, April 1968

Peter Lyman and Hal R. Varian, "How much information?" A study of how much information is produced in the world each year. University of California, Berkeley, October 2000 http://www.sims.berkeley.edu/research/projects/how-much-info/summary.html

Vincent H. Resh, "Science and Communication: An Author/Editor/User's Perspective on the Transition from Paper to Electronic Publishing," Department of Environmental Science, Policy and Management, University of California, Berkeley, summer 1998

Gary Taubes, "Science journals go wired," *Science* magazine, February 9, 1996, p.764

Carol Tenopir and Donald W. King, "Designing Electronic Journals: With 30 Years of Lessons from Print," *The Journal of Electronic Publishing*, December 1998, Volume 4, Issue 2

Hal R. Varian, *The Evolution of Journals: The Future of Electronic Journals*, University of California, Berkeley, 1997. http://www.press.umich.edu/jep/04-01/varian.html

THE BENEFITS AND COSTS OF CONTENT

2

"Lack of efficient publishing capabilities for digital content costs organizations $750 billion annually due to wasted time spent by knowledge workers seeking and capturing information necessary for them to do their jobs."

A.T. Kearney, Network Publishing study, April 2001

Knowledge capital – often called intellectual capital – is more important to the success of a modern organization than physical capital. But while there is broad awareness among managers of knowledge capital's importance, there is little understanding of the manner in which it exists within the organization, or of the way that it is transferred within an organization over time. There is also little understanding of the costs that creating and transferring knowledge capital entails.

This chapter will sketch out a general model to help you measure the benefits and costs of content. It will use broad strokes to create this model, as the processes involved with content are organization-specific, and can become extremely complex. However, it will offer you key measures by which you can fashion a content strategy you can use to increase your share of knowledge capital, and thus increase the value of your bottom line.

"Knowledge capital predicts market performance with more accuracy than does either operating cash flow or net earnings," *CFO Magazine* wrote in 2000. "Managing knowledge capital will be critical for organizations to create a sustainable, competitive advantage," *CFO* quotes Harvard University accounting professor Robert Kaplan as stating. "Today, the long-term success of organizations comes from their knowledge-based assets: customer relationships; innovative products and services; operationally excellent processes; the skills, capabilities, and motivation of their people; and their databases and information systems."

Knowledge capital exists in two forms. First, it exists within the minds of the people who know something useful that will make the organization more productive. Knowledge capital in this form is in essence the collective knowledge of the people who have worked for the organization and those who still do.

In its second form, knowledge capital exists as content. In this sense, content is the formal "written-down" expression of knowledge capital. Once knowledge capital has been turned into content it becomes far more useful – and valuable – to the modern organization.

The classic way knowledge capital was created and transferred within an industrial economy was through apprenticeship models. Young workers gained their knowledge through working with older "knowledge" workers. There is no better way to gain knowledge than through learning by asking, watching, doing.

However, the apprenticeship model has been in decline for at least the past 30 years. One reason for its decline is that it is an expensive way to transfer knowledge. It requires a relatively large workforce of both experienced and apprentice workers, and it depends upon a supply of apprentices prepared to work for several years on a low salary. Younger workers today have a much greater expectation for what they will earn.

Another reason for the decline of the apprenticeship model is that it is most useful when the knowledge being transferred remains stable over a long period of time. When the knowledge base is constantly and rapidly evolving, the value of the experience that an older worker can pass on is reduced.

The increasingly rapid turnover of staff has undermined the apprenticeship model. Whereas in the traditional organization a worker would have been proud to say that they had been with the company for 10 years, now many people feel that if they are not moving on every three years they are losing out.

Finally, the apprenticeship model works well where the organization is centered on a few physical locations. Where the units of production are scattered not just physically but through partners and outsourcing activities – as has been the case increasingly in recent decades – the model is less useful.

The new model for the transfer of knowledge is the content model. Successful organizations need to become proficient at creating and perfecting this model. Content is *the* key resource of the information economy – the key way that knowledge capital is created and articulated today.

Strangely, the true benefits and costs of content are very poorly understood and measured within most organizations. The discipline of knowledge management has sought to bring a more scientific view to content – to how knowledge is created and managed, but there is little real success so far. Organizations have a warm fuzzy feeling about content. They know it is important. Many managers recognize that content is critical. Few know how to go about professionally measuring this critical resource.

Content is indispensable to the information organization. In a study of content in academia – the ultimate knowledge industry, if you think about it – Tenopir and King (1998) stated that, "We found abundant evidence that scholarly journals are not only widely read, but are extremely useful and important to scientists' work, whether it be teaching, research, administration, or other activities. Furthermore, the value of the information is clearly established, whether measured by what users are willing to pay for it (purchase value) or by the benefits derived from its use (use value)."

Tribal societies valued hunter-gatherer skills. Agricultural societies valued land. Industrial societies valued factories. Information societies value content. It's as simple as that. Today, content increasingly drives the "value" of the organization and the individual. Tomorrow, it will drive that value even more. By and large, those who are good at content will prosper. Those who are not will perish.

Content benefits commerce

In 1971, the American publishing executive Merle Hinrichs launched a series of trade magazines in Asia. These magazines helped Western buyers find out about what Asian manufacturers were selling. In 2000, Hinrichs' company, Global Sources, made $62 million in advertising and subscription revenue. It was a simple formula. Asian companies had the goods; Western buyers had the markets. Hinrichs created the bridge with content. He understood the value of quality content to business. When *Forbes* magazine asked him what he thought of the Internet, his reply was, "The Web was like manna from heaven."

Often, we don't realize the true power that quality content has. (Equally, we don't realize the negative potential of poor content.) In the new economy, content will increasingly be the difference between making and not making that sale. Commerce is selling with people. E-commerce is selling with content.

I go to an automotive website not in search of a salesman, much less to buy a car, but rather for *content* about cars. The website informs me about the price, the features, the availability of such and such a model. It informs me what colors I can choose from. It tells me if leather seats are available in that model, and, if so, how much extra they cost. It allows me to read customer reviews. It may even be interactive, allowing me to look at a specific model in different colors and different configurations. It gives me the right content that helps me make the right decision. (At least that's what my ideal car website would do!)

Will I buy my car from a website? Probably not. Does that mean the Web has failed, has not delivered value? Absolutely not! A quality website has delivered real benefit. It has made me more knowledgeable about cars and influenced the purchase decision I will ultimately make. The Web has supported the purchase process. Its content has filled in some vital knowledge gaps for me. Ideally, it has moved me along the curve to a point where I am now more ready to purchase.

The fact that people who use the Web see it as a way to become better informed before they make a purchase is well illustrated by a Gartner survey published in 2000. The survey found that between September 1999 and March 2000, 45 percent of US households that bought a new vehicle used the Internet to research their purchase. Only 3 percent, however, actually bought their vehicle online. A 2000 worldwide survey by American Express found that while 28 percent of respondents expected to shop online, 70 percent said they would use the Web for research purposes, while making the actual purchase in a real store.

> **A survey in 2000 found that between September 1999 and March 2000, 45 percent of US households that bought a new vehicle used the Internet to research their purchase. Only 3 percent, however, actually bought their vehicle online.**

The use of the Web to deliver value by supporting the sales process is understood by leading organizations. Dell Computers has found that people who have visited its website make fewer phone calls to Dell before they purchase a computer than other customers. Not only is Dell selling more computers because of the Web, but the cost of goods sold is reduced because telesales staff need to spend less time convincing a prospective customer. Dell understands that the right Web content delivered to the right person at the right time drives more sales, reduces costs and enhances profit. That's real value.

Customers value quality service. If they find the right content quickly at a website, they will view that as quality service. If they spend ages searching for a piece of content and then find that it's out of date, they will not be happy. That's like making a customer in an offline store wait for ages for an assistant, only to find that the assistant gives them the wrong information. If organizations realized the true impact that content has on customer loyalty on the Web, there would be much less poor-quality content published.

Content benefits decision-making

"The work of managers, of scientists, of engineers, of lawyers – the work that steers the course of society and its economic and governmental organizations – is largely the work of making decisions and solving problems," Herbert Simon, Nobel Laureate in Science, wrote in 1986. In the past, many organizations made decisions based on experience and gut instinct. If managers wanted information to help them make decisions, they often relied on their professional or social networks. Experience, instinct and good networking will always be central to any decision process. However, on their own they are no longer enough.

Decisions need to be made quickly but they need to be informed decisions. To make the right decision there is often an information gap. This gap is increasingly being bridged by content. Of course, a critical problem that a modern manager faces is not too little content, but rather too much.

While information overload is one of the key challenges that an information organization faces, it partly reflects an economy that is increasingly run on content. The right content to the right manager at the right time makes for a more efficient and profitable organization. It makes for better decisions, made faster.

Content benefits staff loyalty and organizational cohesion

Content can benefit staff satisfaction and loyalty. Getting and keeping quality staff is an increasingly important function of the modern organization. Quality content describes for a potential employee what the organization does, what products it has, what sort of philosophy and work atmosphere it has. An iLogos Research study found that in 2000 almost 80 percent of the world's top 500 companies now recruit new staff on their corporate websites, up from 29 percent in 1998.

Quality content also attracts quality people who wish to improve their knowledge while with the organization. In academia, a key way to attract the best professors is by having a substantial library. If the organization has a content-rich intranet, this will attract quality people.

Few organizations realize the importance of an intranet for the day-to-day articulation of strategy and for organizational cohesion. For a physically dispersed organization, the intranet is probably the only place that every member of the organization can see every working day. Many organizations are having great difficulty in communicating a common strategy and approach. An intranet full of rich content will not solve that problem, but it can certainly support the broader and more effective communication of strategy.

Content benefits innovation and learning

Those who invented what would become the Internet had a revolutionary idea. Until the Internet came along the computer was essentially seen as something disassociated from human thinking. It was not seen as a way to develop new knowledge and new ideas. Rather, the ideas were hatched in minds, discussed in rooms, and then input into computers to be processed, stored or tested.

These functions carried out by computers were very valuable, but the inventors of the Internet sought to take things further. They aimed to help people develop better ideas. They wanted to give people a tool to communicate and share ideas in a more efficient manner so that these ideas could be more quickly and comprehensively explored, expanded and widened.

If commerce is selling with people, and e-commerce is selling with content, then learning is teaching with people, and e-learning is teaching with content. Content does not simply deliver learning through specific learning courses. Content underlies the whole principle of life-long learning. As we saw in the previous chapter, those academics who read more got more awards, including higher pay.

Classroom-based learning can have exceptional power if you have a good teacher. However, because what a member of staff needs to learn is changing so quickly, often it is simply not practical nor cost-effective to be continuously getting people into rooms. In such situations, content benefits learning. Content will never replace the power of human interaction, but it is a lot better than nothing.

THE COST OF CONTENT

It all sounds so wonderful. Let's have lots of content. But it's never that easy. Publishing quality content is an expensive process because it takes the time and the thinking of quality people – and they don't come cheap.

FIGURE 2.1

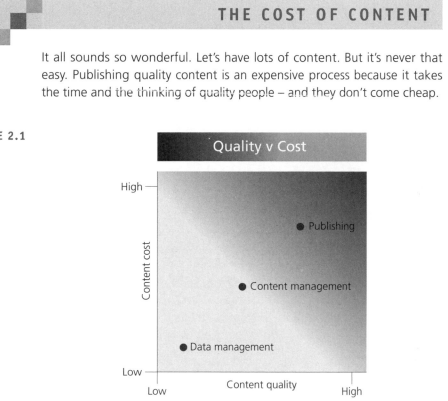

As with all business decisions, there is a classic trade-off at play between the quality of content and the associated costs. Data management is a relatively cheap way to manage content, though mixed quality is the result. Publishing delivers concise, readable content, but the processes to achieve this are expensive. Better ways to measure the real benefits of content need to be developed, so that this trade-off can be more professionally managed.

Too many organizations still look at content as a commodity. The tools for measuring and managing how content is created, edited and published are primitive. The understanding of the benefits and costs of content among a great many managers is equally primitive. We are really only scratching the surface of developing professional publishing processes and standards for content.

Content is costly to create, edit and publish

There is a myth that the Web will make the publishing of content extremely cheap. This ignores the fact that creating quality content is very labor-intensive, resulting in a high fixed cost. A Web-based content management system can have a substantial impact on the workflow costs for publishing content by refining the processes involved. It will not, however, substantially reduce the amount of time it takes to think of the idea and write it down properly.

Looking again at the academic organization, according to Tenopir and King (1997), the "first-copy" costs of an academic article are between $2,000 and $4,000. These costs are mainly made up from the cost of labor involved in the creation, administration, submission, review, editing, type-setting and layout of the document.

For the average academic journal, Varian (1997) estimates that the fixed cost is in the region of $120,000 per year, with a variable cost of printing and distribution of $12 per copy. What this means is that unless you have a high subscription base, the fixed cost of publication is by far the major outlay.

On the surface, the distribution cost of Web content is negligible, because there is no distribution! Rather, the reader comes to the website. However, this ignores an important benefit of distribution – promotion. A fundamental role of distribution is to promote the publication to the reader. That's why newspapers, for example, try to achieve as wide a distribution as possible. You go to the shop to buy some milk, see an interesting headline in a paper, and decide to buy it. Without wide distribution and prominent display, far fewer newspapers would be sold. An increasing challenge of the Web publisher is, "How do I let my reader know about the great document I've just published?"

There are more than fixed, printing and distribution costs to be considered. Cooper (1989) estimated that the archiving or storage cost of a

A reason the Web is in such a mess at the moment is because so little effort is spent on archiving. People have dumped their content on the Web without bothering to take the time to add the correct metadata.

single copy of a journal in a library can run anywhere from $25 to $40. This is a critical Web publishing cost. Adding metadata (information about the author, the date of publication, the classification, etc.) is in essence an approach to professionally archiving documents so that they can be more easily found by readers. A reason the Web is in such a mess at the moment is because so little effort is spent on archiving. People have dumped their content on the Web without bothering to take the time to add the correct metadata. The result is overload and chaos.

Think for a moment of that report on your desk. Supposing nobody reads it because it couldn't be found due to poor archiving. That's $4,000 down the drain. If a factory makes tables and nobody buys them, the factory will stop production. Because the cost and benefit of content is so poorly understood, content that is never read keeps getting created.

Lesk (1997) reported that 22 percent of science papers, 48 percent of social science papers and an incredible 93 percent of humanities papers published in 1984 were not quoted over the next 10 years. The fact that your document wasn't referred to in another document doesn't necessarily mean that it wasn't read. However, it does indicate that even if it was read, it didn't have much of an impact. Content is "written down" information. If information doesn't inform, doesn't communicate knowledge, what good is it?

Content is difficult to create, edit and publish

The dirty little secret of the Web is that the majority of content published ranges from poor to downright awful. Whether unpublished authors like it or not, the reason why publishers reject up to 90 percent of the manuscripts they receive is because most of them are of poor quality.

Information literacy is not simply about writing well. Before you can write well you have to be able to read well. Tenopir and King (1998) found that reading made academics more productive and saved them an average of $300 per article read. "Savings are said to result from avoiding having to do some primary research; stopping an unproductive line of research; or modifying research, analysis, or engineering design." They also found that those who read more progressed more. "In one company," they wrote, "twenty-five scientists who were considered particularly high achievers read 59 percent more articles than the other scientists."

Content processes are difficult to automate

The Achilles Heel of technology is its often blind belief that with the right line of code everything can be automated. This is the most fundamental mistake that modern organizations make with regard to technology. They try to use it to solve problems it cannot solve, to do things it cannot do. The result is that by asking technology to do what it cannot do – think up and publish great ideas – the organization wastes time and money and delivers poor results.

In time, machines that can think up great ideas and write them down well may evolve. That day is not with us (thankfully). People think. People write. Computers facilitate that thinking. Only a fool would trust a word processor alone to automatically check and change their spelling and grammar. Only a bigger fool thinks that there's software out there that takes poor ideas, poorly written and turns them into great content.

The Internet can *help* people come up with better ideas and get these ideas down as great content. The Internet can support more efficient publishing processes. But it's the classic "garbage in, garbage out" mantra; no amount of clever processes will turn poor writing into good writing. The 550 billion-plus documents on intranets, extranets and Internet websites today merely inform us of how many awful publishers there are.

Content is difficult to organize

Organizing content is not easy. The more there is, the more complex it gets. Content that is not well organized is difficult to find. This is an increasingly costly problem facing organizations today.

Search is a non-productive publishing activity. It is something we do when we're lost. Getting 10,000 results from a search is not something that excites the average person. Jakob Nielsen, a usability expert, has stated that, "users almost never look beyond the second page of search results."

Classifying content in a logical manner that is intuitive from a reader's perspective is a major challenge that many organizations have failed to meet. We see the emergence of information architecture as a discipline to address content organization needs, but we are really only scratching the surface of a most complex task. In essence, information architecture addresses information overload.

Some hope that there is magical software out there that will solve the content organization challenge. Software may be part of the solution but without skilled people who understand both the content needs of the organization and the reader, little will be achieved. Organizing content will become an increasingly important and costly activity for the information organization.

Content is difficult to measure

There is a simple rule in the commercial publishing world. If it doesn't sell you don't get paid. In academic and literary publishing, the rules are not so stringent. Some writers are happy to publish to small readerships because their work is specialized. These writers accept that they will make very little money out of publishing.

In a commercial environment, every piece of content should make a profit, either directly or indirectly. However, very few organizations have a clue as to what part of their content is profitable and what is not. The basic ability to measure the benefit and cost of content is either primitive or non-existent.

The historical remuneration principle for business is pay per hour worked. In publishing it is pay per word. If an author is writing a book, they are asked to deliver a certain number of words within a certain time-frame. The same applies to articles. The problem in today's organization is that staff are expected to write up reports, technical papers and other documents, almost as a side-product of their real job.

A second approach to remuneration is largely made possible because of the Internet. It involves measuring how many people have read the document, or how many have referred to or linked to it.

The benefits and costs of content are difficult to measure precisely. That does not mean they cannot be measured. In fact, it is vital to establish a cost-benefit model for content, otherwise it will be managed in an ad-hoc manner. Here, we sketch out a general, top-level model for content benefit, and a more detailed model for measuring content costs.

Modeling content benefits

Knowledge, content and information map well to the three key publishing processes: creation, editing, publishing. Creation is about tapping into knowledge for a particular idea or set of ideas. Editing is about turning those ideas into professional content. Publishing is about getting that content to the right person at the right time. To generate content benefit, you need to create, edit and publish. Thus, content benefit has a simple formula:

Content benefit = create X edit X publish

It is important to note that calculating content benefit involves multiplication rather than addition. To illustrate the multiplier effect, let's say you have 30 hours available to create content benefit. If you spend 15 on thinking up a great idea (create), and 15 editing that idea into great content (edit), but you don't have any time left to actually publish the content, what would be your content benefit? It would be:

15 X 15 X 0 = 0

Not publishing your content would be like printing up 100,000 magazines and leaving them in the corner of your office. We should look at the above formula as indicative, but as a general rule you need to pay equal attention to create, edit and publish.

In establishing a model for the benefit of content, there are a number of sub-processes which underpin the creation, editing, and publishing processes. All of these need to be optimized if you want to get the maximum benefit from your content. We summarize the benefits of these sub-processes in the following table, but will examine them in greater detail in the rest of the book.

	Publishing processes	Benefits
Create	Identification of reader	The right reader is identified. If the wrong reader is identified, everything else is useless
	Identification of content	The right content is identified for this reader
	Creation	Professionally-created content to commonly-agreed standards
	Commissioning	The right content is commissioned on time and within budget
	Acquisition	The right content is cost-effectively acquired
	Reader-created content	Readers interact, enhancing loyalty and creating cost-effective content
Edit	Contribution	Proper metadata ensures content is properly classified and directed to the right editor
	Editing	Content professionally edited
	Review	Out-of-date content removed
	Correcting	Libelous or illegal content quickly removed

Publish	Publishing	Content presented professionally in a timely manner can be found quickly
	Subscription-based publishing	Reader receives the right content on a regular basis
	Reader interaction	Readers are responded to in a professional and timely manner
	Promotion	The right reader is informed of the publication of the right content
Manage	Measurement	All processes are correctly measured for performance
	Training	The organization is trained in the correct publishing skills

Modeling content costs

There are a great many costs involved with content and a formula that would measure each one would be very long. It would also depend on so many and such complex variables that it is highly likely that the cost in time of working out the formula would outweigh its benefits.

What we propose to do here is isolate some of the more measurable processes involved in publishing content and to establish a basic cost model that will prove useful to managers who wish to broadly track what their content is costing them to publish.

The first step in creating such a model is to establish a basic unit for content. This we call a document. A document is a unique unit of content that can contain text, images and/or numbers. (We are not dealing with video and audio documents of content in this book.) Documents, of course, can be long or short. However, for simplicity we are assuming that over a yearly period, documents will average out at the same size.

To illustrate a cost model for content let us model one of the sub-processes in publishing content: contribution. The "contribute" process involves preparing the document for submission to the editor. Much of the contribute process involves putting metadata around the document. The first element in the formula is the time it takes to contribute the document. The next element is the hourly cost of the person charged with contributing it. The formula is thus relatively simple:

No of documents X time to contribute X cost of contributor = cost of contribution

Let's say it takes 15 minutes to contribute the document, and the contributor is paid $40 an hour. The formula would thus be:

1 X .25 X 40 = $10

Using the above formula on any of our publishing processes we can establish core costs of publishing a particular document. The organization that wants to publish content cost-effectively can then work to reduce the number of rejected documents and streamline the process to save time.

Search cost

Those who seek to cut corners on their creation, contribution or editing costs will likely pay the price with regard to how quick it is to find the content and how easy it is to read it. Prolonged search means that the right content is not getting to the right person at the right time. For the information worker, it is a frustrating and time-consuming experience. For the information consumer it means that they're not getting quickly to the content that will help them buy the product.

Lost productivity through search can quickly mount up. As we read in the introductory quote to this chapter, a 2001 study published by A.T. Kearney estimates that poor publishing processes relating to the searching for and capturing of content will cost organizations $750 billion annually.

Let's say there are 50 people in your organization. Let's say they spend on average six minutes every day searching for content (6/60 minutes is equal to .1). Let's say the average cost per person is $40 per hour. Based on a 250-day working year, the following formula would apply:

50 X .1 X $40 X 250 = $50,000

$50,000 relates to the lost productivity as a result of search. If you have 1,000 people working in your organization, the search cost rises to

$1 million. Taking one minute off the six-minute search time would reduce your search costs by almost $170,000 over a 12-month period.

Search costs do not simply apply to your staff looking for content on an intranet. They also very much apply to your customer searching for product information on your public website. If you are wasting their time with a poorly designed publication, you might as well be charging them more for the product you are offering them. Because wasting their time is wasting their money.

Time-to-publish cost

If competitors keep getting their content on their product up on their website quicker than you, then – all else being equal – they will gain market share over you.

Time-to-publish is one of the most critical costs that a modern organization faces. If competitors keep getting products into the shops before you do, then – other things being equal – they will gain market share over you. If your competitor keeps getting their content on their product up on their website quicker than you, then – all else being equal – they will gain market share over you.

The best way to illustrate the cost of time-to-publish is with an example. Supposing your new product has a fault. You prepare the fix. The next step is to get that fix to all the customers who bought the product. You could mail that fix to all your customers but that might be overly expensive and slow. You could wait for frustrated customers to telephone. Alternatively, you could publish content on the fix on your website, and perhaps notify your customers by email. The quicker you do that the more chance you have of reducing support calls. Reducing support calls saves you money.

Promotion cost

Without constant promotion, nobody knows your website is there. This is the flip-side of the Web's close-to-zero distribution costs. Close-to-zero distribution costs may also equate to close-to-zero readers.

We are not proposing a formula here as it would simply be too difficult to measure. It's like that famous complaint of Philadelphia department-store magnate John Wanamaker – "I know that half the money I spend on advertising is wasted; but I can never find out which half." However, it is safe to say that if you have a zero budget for promoting your content, you will likely have a greatly reduced readership.

Readership cost

We thought we'd save the best wine till last. The most critical factor in the cost of publishing is both the type and number of readers. As we have seen earlier, much of the cost of creating a particular document of content is fixed. This "first copy" cost has critical implications in any publishing environment. If you have a small number of readers the cost per reader is very high.

If the cost per reader is very high then you need to establish the benefit of delivering this content to this reader. The benefit must outweigh the cost. Otherwise, you're publishing at a loss. As Varian (1997) pointed out, the fixed cost of an academic publication was $120,000 per year, with a variable cost of printing and distribution of $12 per copy. With a readership of 1,000, the break-even point would be $132, with $12 of this being the variable cost and $120 being the fixed cost. If the readership was 10,000, the break-even point would be $24; $12 fixed and $12 variable.

The cost savings of publishing on the Internet are thus illusory unless the readership is optimized. Let's say for a moment that variable publishing costs on the Web are zero. However, because we have not distributed our publication to bookstores, libraries, etc., the readership is 500, instead of the 1,000 mentioned. Our break-even cost would now be $240, instead of $132.

Content is critical to the modern organization. It is how the organization increasingly communicates and derives value from its intellectual capital. However, content is poorly understood, measured and managed within organizations today. Managing content professionally is an essential skill that organizations and their staffs must acquire if they want to be successful in an information economy.

The Web allows for more efficient and cost-effective publishing processes. However, because the "first copy" cost of a document of content is very substantial, readership reach is important to the success of any publication. If you are reaching fewer people with a Web publication than with a print one, Web publishing will be less effective and quite probably more expensive. After all, if the Web is such a great publishing medium, why haven't newspaper, magazine and book publishers stopped using print?

References

Marjolien Bot, Johan Burgemeester and Hans Tilburg Roes, "The Cost of Publishing an Electronic Journal: A general model and a case study," University Library D-Lib Magazine, November 1998

CFO magazine, "The Second Annual Knowledge Capital Scoreboard: A Knowing Glance," February 2000

Michael D. Cooper, "A Cost Comparison of Alternative Book Storage Strategies," *Library Quarterly*, July 1989

A.T. Kearney, *Network Publishing: Creating value through digital content*, April 2001 http://www.atkearney.com/main.taf?site=1&a=1&b=5&c=1&d=75

Michael Lesk, "Books, Bytes and Bucks: Practical Digital Libraries," TBA, San Francisco, 1997

Andrew Odlyzko, *The Economics of Electronic Journals* first Monday, August 1997

Carol Tenopir and Donald W. King, "Trends in Scientific Scholarly Journal Publishing in the United States," *Journal of Scholarly Publishing*, April 1997

Carol Tenopir and Donald W. King, "Designing Electronic Journals: With 30 Years of Lessons from Print," *The Journal of Electronic Publishing*, December 1998, Volume 4, Issue 2

Carol Tenopir and Donald W. King, *Economic Cost Models of Scientific Scholarly Journals*, University of Tennessee School of Information Sciences, Center for Information Studies, April 1998

Hal R. Varian, *The Evolution of Journals: The Future of Electronic Journals*, 1997

THE READER IS KING

3

In business the customer is king. On the Internet, we hear that "content is king." But that's like saying from a business perspective that "product is king." It's the exact opposite of what "customer is king" thinking is about. If the customer is king in business then the customer (reader) is king on the Internet.

If the reader is king then content serves the reader. Thus, from a business perspective, the purpose of content is to deliver quality information to the reader that will help further the organization's objectives. Readers need a reason to visit and re-visit the website, and must feel they have learned something as a result. When appropriate, content must create a "call to action" for readers, getting them to purchase the organization's products or services. Above all, content should make the reader think better of the organization as a result of reading the content.

Publishers who don't make the reader king go out of business. A classic fault of writing and publishing is that it puts the ego of the author or editor before the needs of the reader. If you don't write for the reader then the reader won't read you. If the reader doesn't read you you don't have a business model.

It's a strange and fascinating thing how easily content gets disassociated from its reader. There are billions of documents on the Internet today. A great many of them were not written with a reader in mind. They are boring, too long, verbose, incoherent, misleading, out-of-date, unreadable.

The publication process begins and ends with the reader. Technical issues are a sideshow. Unfortunately, the technology is a sideshow that has for too long hogged center stage when it comes to how organizations have dealt with the Internet. Understanding your reader is much more important than understanding technology. At every step of the way, keep the following simple questions in mind:

- Who is my reader?
- Will they read this?
- What value is being created?

Get the reader right and you are halfway there. Get the reader wrong and you are on the slippery slope to nowhere.

Publishing skills are far more important than publishing technology. It would be better to have 500 words of the right content handwritten on scrap paper, delivered by snail mail, than to have 5,000 words of waffle sent by high-speed wireless to your mobile phone.

Unfortunately, the current focus has been very much on the technology, with a general lack of focus on developing key publishing skills. According to Ross Dawson, chief executive of Advanced Human Technologies, an Australian knowledge management consultancy, "Individual information and knowledge skills – which include filtering information overload, effective reading, note-taking, analysis, synthesis and communicating effectively to others – have rarely been deliberately developed."

Barth (2000) states that, "In attempting to apply their collective expertise for competitive advantage, corporations often overlook the fundamental truth that knowledge begins and ends as personal. Without human understanding, personal context and immediate utility, all we have is data."

Literacy used to be about basic reading and writing. No longer. The International Adult Literacy Survey defines literacy as, "The ability to understand and employ printed information in daily activities, at home, at work, and in the community – to achieve one's goals and to develop one's knowledge and potential." According to the American Library Association, "Ultimately, information-literate people are those who have learned how to learn. They know how to learn because they know how knowledge is organized, how to find information, and how to use information in such a way that others can learn from them."

Consider the following:

- According to a 2000 study by Campus Pipeline, American students see the Web as their second most important resource when deciding what college to go to (the first is their guidance counselors).

- A study by Keen.com and Lewis, Mobilio & Associates found that Americans ask an average of four questions per day, and spend an average of 8.75 hours per week searching for answers. The Internet has become the top resource for finding these answers.

- A 2000 report by the OECD entitled, "Literacy in the information age," stated that, "Workers are increasingly required not only to have higher levels of education, but also the capacity to adapt, learn and master the changes quickly and efficiently."

Skills of the information literate

All of us – whether we are workers, managers or consumers – require new skills for the new economy. This economy increasingly runs on content. If we are consumers of content, then we need to be able to figure out what content we need, go out and find it, and then put it to practical use. In the process, we need to be able to deal with information overload, and not get smothered by it. If we are publishers of content, we need to be able to create, edit and publish content in the most professional manner possible.

The information-literate have these characteristics and skills:

- They read a lot, are hungry for new ideas and are always inquisitive. They talk, discuss and collaborate a lot, and they write a lot. They have the ability to look at a problem and see what sort of information is needed to solve it. They know how to ask the right questions.

- They have strong research skills. They know where to go to find information, and don't depend on a single content source; they are content gatherers. They know how to cope with information overload, and are able to quickly tell good content from bad. They set a reasonable amount of time for their research and they know when they have gathered enough content.

- They write well, and know who they're writing for. They have the ability to synopsize what they have found and turn it into new content. They have the skills and desire to collaborate with others in the creation of new content. They have good keyboard skills and can work to deadline.

- They are able to turn their content into persuasive presentations, and are comfortable making presentations in front of a group.

- In addition to these skills, managers and editors of information-literate workers must know how to commission new content and be able quickly to judge its quality. They must know how to manage writers – to encourage them and get the best out of them. They must know how to select the most exciting and relevant content and position it appropriately on the homepage.

People read online in a different way to how they read a newspaper, magazine or book. People "read" newspapers by looking at images first. What this means is that a story with a picture attached is generally more likely to be read than one without. But on the Web it's different. A Stanford University and Poynter Institute study published in 2000 on the habits of people who read news on the Internet asked and answered the question, "Where do eyes go initially after firing up the first screenful of online news? To read text, most likely. Not to photos or graphics, as you might expect."

The Internet and computer screens still represent relatively awkward technology. It's harder to look at things on a screen than in a magazine. Research by Sun Microsystems (1998) found that reading from computer screens is 25 per cent slower than from paper. A visual image looks much better in high resolution on a 28-in television than in lower resolution on a 14-in laptop screen, and vastly better on the page of a glossy magazine.

Many have assumed that the problem of onscreen readability will be solved as bandwidth increases. But the prospect of unlimited bandwidth is still very much a dream for the average Internet reader. Studies estimate that even by 2005, the average reader will not have broadband (high bandwidth) access.

> **People are under a lot of pressure today. We live in the age of information overload. Whether reading on the Web or in a newspaper, the average reader doesn't have the time for content that doesn't get to the point.**

People are also under a lot of pressure today. We live in the age of information overload. Whether reading on the Web or in a newspaper, the average reader doesn't have the time for content that doesn't get to the point.

The Web is a very functional place. The behavior of online readers reflects this reality:

- They are practical and impatient. They come to the Web wanting to find out something. They want to gather content, perhaps from several websites to be able to solve a problem. They quickly want to find what they are looking for.

- They are conservative. Numerous studies have shown that the online reader frequents very few websites. For example, Nielsen NetRatings found that the average person using the Internet in January 2001 visited no more than 19 websites in the entire month. The reason for this conservative behavior is because the Web is so huge and so chaotic, that readers tend to look for branded websites that meet their content needs and then stick with them.

- They are skeptical. Everyone is a publisher on the Internet so anything can get published. Readers have become very wary. If a website doesn't quickly win their confidence, they're gone; probably never to return.

- They are fickle. It costs the reader very little to leave your website. With most offline publications the reader invests money by actually buying them. Thus, readers feel a certain obligation to get their money's worth by reading them. The reader feels no such obligation on the Web.

- They "scan-read." Readers move quickly through text trying to grab the salient points. The Sun Microsystems study in 1998 found that 79 percent of online readers regularly scan-read.

- They don't particularly like reading online, as screen-based reading is not the most comfortable way to read. They particularly don't like movement on the screen, as this makes text very hard to read and hurts their eyes.

- They are not simply at your website to search for a particular piece of information. They also want your opinion on what they should be reading.

In the remainder of this chapter, we'll look in more detail at seven things readers want from your website:

1. Readers want to be able to find things

"Internet access may vary greatly from country to country, but consumers around the globe reveal strikingly similar practices, plans and perspectives when it comes to the burgeoning new online medium," according to a 2000 American Express global internet survey which questioned of 11,410 internet users and non-users in 10 countries.

FIGURE 3.1

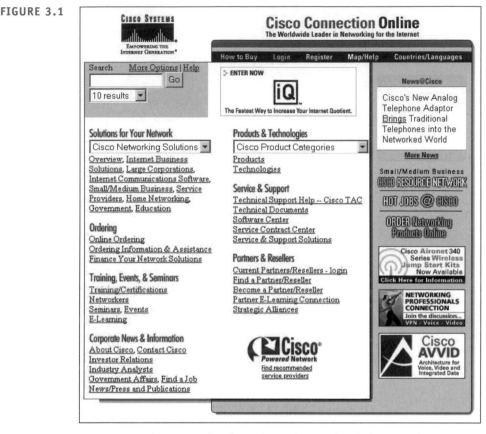

Cisco is a perfect example of a website designed with functionality in mind. The search is prominent, and much of the rest of the homepage is taken up with links that let the reader quickly get to the content they need.

So what does the global internet consumer mainly use the Internet for? "Email communication (74 percent) and information gathering (73 percent) are, by far, the most predominant applications of the Internet," the American Express survey states.

Your readers are in a hurry. The most precious commodity to them is their time. When they come to your website looking for content, they want to find it as quickly as possible. The longer it takes them to find what they are looking for the more dissatisfied they become.

Readers look for content in two ways – through using a search process, and/or by browsing through a classification/navigation system. Using a search process is helpful if they know exactly what they are looking for, but the quality of search offerings on most websites ranges from poor to dismal. A 2000 survey by Roper Starch found that 86 percent of respondents felt that a more efficient way to search the Web for accurate content should be available.

The reader does not always have a particular document in mind when they are visiting a website. A 2000 study by Xerox Palo Alto Research Center found that only 25 percent of respondents had a specific piece of content in mind when they used the Web; 75 percent came to the Web to find out about something and/or to gather content on a specific subject. This is a critical point to understand and a fundamental difference between how organizations have traditionally approached content, and how they need to approach it on the Web.

The reader, for example, may want to find out information on Ireland, on computer notebooks, on mobile phones. For the reader to be satisfied, content must have been properly classified so that on a particular website, all the content on notebooks for example, is in the same place and is well organized. Proper classification of content gives the reader context as they seek to gather information. It is a foundation stone upon which a professional Web publication is built.

We want a publication to deliver an opinion on what's important, and we are drawn to publications that reflect in a substantive way our interests and our views on life.

Another unique tool that the Web offers is personalization. Properly done, personalization can help readers find the content they need more quickly. Personalization is about discerning the reading habits of your readers and delivering to them just the content they're after. It's a delicate, complex and expensive process that is suitable only for websites that have large quantities of content. However, it can be a real benefit by short-cutting the route the reader has to follow to search for that content.

Readers hate websites that take a long time to download. They hate websites that are full of fancy bells and whistles. They hate impediments to finding the content they want. As The Industry Standard put it in February 2000, "While cable modems, DSL and T1 lines have sped things up, many sites are still overloaded with graphics, ads and animation that bogs down even the fastest connection... Frustrated by the eternally slow Internet, tech-savvy news junkies are peeling away websites to get to the juice: words."

For a great many people, the Web is a bread-and-butter operation. They're not there for the fun; they're there for the content. A 2001 study by Lyra Research found that more than 60 percent of respondents chose the Internet for personal information needs, as against 18 percent who looked to magazines for such information. For work-related information, 48 percent chose the Internet, with only 7 percent choosing magazines. More and more, the Internet is where people come to *know*.

They want to know quickly. Studies have shown that you will lose up to one-third of your readers if your web pages take 10 seconds or more to download. What this all calls for is a minimal graphical design layout for your content. On the Internet, design complexity is in how the content is organized, not in the visual graphics. More often than not, graphics just get in the way.

Helping the reader quickly find the content they want has clear benefits. Nortel Networks estimates that as a result of properly organizing its content, each member of its sales staff saves an average of two minutes every day searching for documents. That adds up to $10 million in savings every year.

2. Readers want your advice

Practically all successful publications deliver a point of view – or offer their readers some guidance about what to read. Some publications may state that they deliver "just the facts." Facts, however, are invariably colored by the attitudes of those who write them, and, anyway, most of us are too busy to assemble and evaluate all the facts. We want a publication to deliver an opinion on what's important, and we are drawn to publications that reflect in a substantive way our interests and our views on life.

Early views about the Web were of a giant store of content that provided you with powerful search engines and then left you to "search" out what you wanted. Search is an important activity. It is something you do when you have a very specific need, when you know exactly what you are looking for. Search is also something you do when you're lost. Most of us don't like being lost.

A classic example of the difference between search and opinion is the differing approaches that Yahoo and Alta Vista took in supplying content options to their readers. Alta Vista believed in the ultimate power of technology. It took a "search engine" approach. Its software gathered as many websites as it could find and then gave the reader a powerful search facility. Alta Vista was all about giving the reader unlimited choice.

FIGURE 3.2

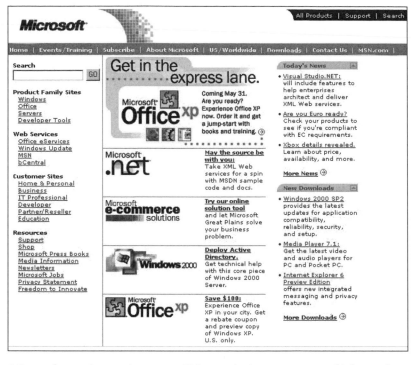

Microsoft sure knows how to sell! It uses its homepage as a "Microsoft Daily," providing opinion and telling the reader about all the great things it has to offer today.

Yahoo is not a search engine. It is, rather, a directory publisher. Instead of sending out software to index the Web, it commissioned editors to judge which were the best websites, and offered its readers "limited" choice. Many more readers came to Yahoo than to Alta Vista.

The reader does not want to be bombarded by an unlimited choice. Publishing is as much about what you don't publish as what you do. (Yahoo publishes links to less than 6 percent of the websites on the Internet.) It is about presenting to a time-starved, information-overloaded reader a select set of content. Online readers want an opinion or guidance on what they should buy, what stocks are the best value, what new products or special offers the organization has. They would like to know what the organization thinks is "news."

All great publications and all great websites have an opinion, a point of view that reflects and is reflected by the uniqueness of the organization's brand and product offering. Having an opinion is what drives sales on the Internet. Why otherwise did Amazon place the new Harry Potter book on its homepage for weeks? Because it knew it would help drive sales.

Having an opinion is about doing the searching for the reader. It's about sifting through the growing mountain of content and delivering to the reader the important bits – the stuff that they should read today. A newspaper puts its most important story of the day on its front page. A website publication, whether it's for an intranet or the Internet, should also seek to put its most important story of the day on its homepage. That's what will bring readers and keep them coming back.

3. Readers want up-to-date, quality content

Some rules are so obvious you'd think that everyone would follow them. Yet the most obvious rules are often the most frequently broken. The Internet is a highly dynamic medium, in that content can be updated continuously. The reader has therefore come to expect that a website will give them the most up-to-date content available. The best websites are those that have up-to-date content. The worst websites don't.

Having out-of-date content costs money. Anton (2001) states that, "One Fortune 100 firm we've worked with provided paper policy and procedure manuals to support its 40,000 operations personnel. Upon conducting a company-wide audit, this firm concluded it was losing $2 million a day due to mistakes and delays to locate 'how-to' information in their hard copy manuals." The Web should solve this sort of problem. However, a 2000 NOP survey of large UK firms found that 77 percent admitted their websites contained out-of-date content.

Because it's so easy to set up a basic website, practically anyone can be a publisher. What this has led to is millions of websites and billions of web pages. Much of the content that you will find on the Internet is poor quality. Therefore, the online reader has become increasingly skeptical.

It is a major challenge to overcome the reader's skepticism about the quality of online content and how up to date it is. This challenge can be overcome only by publishing quality content each day.

4. Readers want relevant and straightforward content

The content that seems relevant to you is not always what is relevant to your reader. "Less is more" is the motto the organization should follow with regard to publishing content. The reader is busy and starved for time. Don't publish content just because you have it. Only publish content that is relevant.

This is the age of the buzzword. Practically every word is getting an "e" put in front of it. Many organizations have developed their own terminology that they assume their readers (customers) will understand. However, people are tired of convoluted language. If you want to communicate with your reader, start off by writing in language that does not confuse them. Write simply. Write directly. Write concisely. Remember, your reader's in a hurry. Get to the point.

Whatever you do, don't write like the following selection from a major consultancy: "After removing client-sensitive information, we develop 'knowledge objects' by pulling key pieces of knowledge such as interview guides, work schedules, benchmark data, and market segmentation analyses out of documents and storing them in the electronic repository for people to use."

Translated into plain English, "After removing confidential information, we write up reports that we publish on our intranet."

FIGURE 3.3

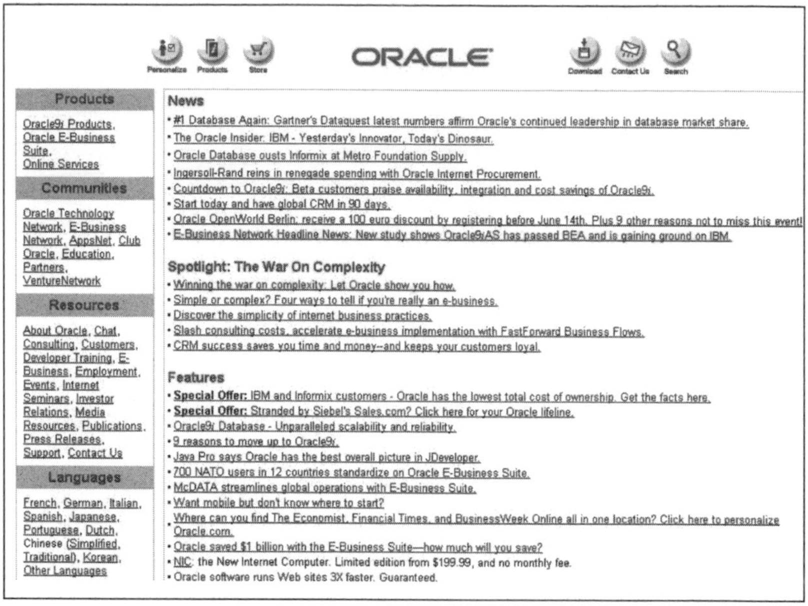

ORACLE

Personalize Products Store   Download Contact Us Search

Products
Oracle9i Products,
Oracle E-Business
Suite,
Online Services

Communities
Oracle Technology
Network, E-Business
Network, AppsNet, Club
Oracle, Education,
Partners,
VentureNetwork

Resources
About Oracle, Chat,
Consulting, Customers,
Developer Training, E-
Business, Employment,
Events, Internet
Seminars, Investor
Relations, Media
Resources, Publications,
Press Releases,
Support, Contact Us

Languages
French, German, Italian,
Spanish, Japanese,
Portuguese, Dutch,
Chinese (Simplified,
Traditional), Korean,
Other Languages

News
- #1 Database Again: Gartner's Dataquest latest numbers affirm Oracle's continued leadership in database market share.
- The Oracle Insider: IBM - Yesterday's Innovator, Today's Dinosaur.
- Oracle Database ousts Informix at Metro Foundation Supply.
- Ingersoll-Rand reins in renegade spending with Oracle Internet Procurement.
- Countdown to Oracle9i: Beta customers praise availability, integration and cost savings of Oracle9i.
- Start today and have global CRM in 90 days.
- Oracle OpenWorld Berlin: receive a 100 euro discount by registering before June 14th. Plus 9 other reasons not to miss this event!
- E-Business Network Headline News: New study shows Oracle9iAS has passed BEA and is gaining ground on IBM.

Spotlight: The War On Complexity
- Winning the war on complexity. Let Oracle show you how.
- Simple or complex? Four ways to tell if you're really an e-business.
- Discover the simplicity of internet business practices.
- Slash consulting costs, accelerate e-business implementation with FastForward Business Flows.
- CRM success saves you time and money--and keeps your customers loyal.

Features
- **Special Offer:** IBM and Informix customers - Oracle has the lowest total cost of ownership. Get the facts here.
- **Special Offer:** Stranded by Siebel's Sales.com? Click here for your Oracle lifeline.
- Oracle9i Database - Unparalleled scalability and reliability.
- 9 reasons to move up to Oracle9i.
- Java Pro says Oracle has the best overall picture in JDeveloper.
- 700 NATO users in 12 countries standardize on Oracle E-Business Suite.
- McDATA streamlines global operations with E-Business Suite.
- Want mobile but don't know where to start?
- Where can you find The Economist, Financial Times, and BusinessWeek Online all in one location? Click here to personalize Oracle.com.
- Oracle saved $1 billion with the E-Business Suite—how much will you save?
- NIC: the New Internet Computer. Limited edition from $199.99, and no monthly fee.
- Oracle software runs Web sites 3X faster. Guaranteed.

The Oracle homepage is nothing if not up-to-date and to the point. It won't win any visual design prizes, but the content effectively communicates that classic Oracle hard sell.

5. Readers want to do things

The Web is a no-frills action-oriented place. The majority of people don't use the Web for fun or to browse casually. They want to find something, to do something. From a business perspective, content can drive revenue in the following ways:

- Directly through the reader paying for the content.
- Indirectly through the content prompting the reader to initiate an action on the website which may lead to a purchase.
- Indirectly through the reader developing a favorable impression of the organization and its products or services.

It's easy-come, easy-go on the Web. Once readers have arrived at your website it is imperative to get some sort of commitment from them. Content is working well when it moves the reader from the passive reading mode towards a positive action mode. Many products and services will not be sold with content alone. Provide the reader with the opportunity to email, telephone, chat, or otherwise interact with the organization.

Initially, readers may not feel they need a direct engagement with the organization. In this situation, one of the best ways of hooking them in is to offer them a subscription service. Tell them that if they like the content they are reading, they can get updated versions of it by subscribing to your email publication. This call to action gives you the reader's email address and perhaps some other personal information. For the reader, this is a minimal engagement that carries little risk.

The Web is what is described as a "pull medium." Even if readers like your content, they still need actively to decide to revisit your website. Email subscription services are a "push medium." Once readers have given you their email address you can regularly send them content. You have made them give you a certain commitment. You can build a stronger relationship from there. Of course, it goes without saying that if readers do subscribe, you had better give them the quality and relevant content you promised.

6. Readers want to interact

"The customer is now a participant in the production process," Alvin Toffler told *Business 2.0* magazine in September 2000. "What's happening is a shift toward consumption in which the lines have blurred between producer and consumer or customer. The customer provides information as to what they want. Without that information, producers create a product that they can't sell and no-one wants. So in more and more complex technological industries, you have the joint teams working together – customer and supplier. The relationship with the customer to the producer is radically changed and enhanced by the Internet."

While the Internet provides an opportunity for much closer interaction between the organization and the reader, often the opposite occurs. Because interaction inevitably involves people, it can be an expensive process. Many organizations have seen the Internet as a place where they can provide "virtual" interactivity.

Virtual interactivity means that when the reader asks a question or provides feedback, they get an automated response from a piece of software. Sometimes the reader is fooled into thinking that they are getting personal attention. Undoubtedly this approach reduces costs and can work in certain circumstances. But there are limits to the types of "relationships" people like to have with pieces of software. No matter how technologically advanced we like to think we are, people still prefer to interact with other people. Consider the following:

Do not believe that the reader is dying to interact with the organization and will do so at every opportunity. A well-designed website will minimize the amount of unnecessary interaction by having content that answers readers' questions.

- More than 40 percent of respondents said they would have more confidence in a site if they could email customer service or a sales representative, while 45 percent said they would visit a site more often if they received a response to an email query within 12 hours, according to an NFO Interactive report published in January 2001.

- "Retailers have a better chance of satisfying customers when they incorporate human values into their online selling strategies," according to a 2000 global study of consumer attitudes conducted by Ernst & Young. The study pointed out that average online industry conversion rates were less than one-third the average of offline retailers.

Do not believe that the reader is dying to interact with the organization and will do so at every opportunity. A well-designed website will minimize the amount of unnecessary interaction by having content that answers readers' questions, and by having a structure that allows them to find that content quickly. However, when readers do feel that they want to get in touch, the facilities must be there to do so. More importantly, the processes and people must be in place to respond effectively to the reader's queries.

Of course, the flip-side of all this is the classic 80–20 rule, whereby 80 percent of your value comes from 20 percent of your customers. Unfortunately, within the 80 percent of less valuable customers and in the wider "tire kicker" world, there are people who love to interact just for the sake of it.

The key thing with interaction is to set the expectation. Make it clear to readers under what conditions they should send an email and what they should expect as a response (and the timeframe for that response). An example of how not to do it is Network Solutions, which provides domain names and other services. It offers telephone and email interaction. Calling them sends you into telephone hell. But if you email them, you get a response which advises you to telephone them.

Another key Web strategy here is to involve the reader in a type of "online community." Successful Web publications tend to be good at getting the reader engaged, either through feedback, reader reviews, discussion, or chat. Zdnet.com uses this approach effectively. At the bottom of most Zdnet articles is a talk-back discussion forum, where readers can add their views to those of the article's author. Where reader feedback is especially interesting, Zdnet turns that feedback into an article of its own. The benefits are clear – the reader feels more engaged with and loyal to the publication, and the publication gets cost-effective content.

In 1999, America Online had some 12,000 staff and some 10,000 volunteers. Many of these volunteers created and managed content on areas that interested them – from subjects as diverse as pop music to cancer research. This "online community" structure is an effective business model for AOL, in that it creates vibrant environments for AOL members to visit and revisit, while filling these environments with content in a very cost-effective way.

If this sounds too good to be true, then in certain cases it is. Because the reader doesn't work for the organization, they are not likely to take orders from it easily. They may accept gentle guidance and may obey broad rules, but they and other readers can quite easily take a discussion in a direction the organization had not intended. Your readers can become your most severe critics, particularly if they feel that you have let them down in some way.

An online community approach needs to deliver clear value both to readers and the organization. Participating and managing a community demands time, the most valuable resource in an information economy. The people who have the least time are generally those whom the organization wishes most to participate. The people who have most time to participate may not always be those with most value to add.

However, if done right, engaging the reader can be the essential difference between a vibrant and cost-effective Web strategy and one which is static and expensive to run. Remember, readers have a desire to act when they're on the Web. It's the job of content to encourage them.

7. Readers want privacy

Survey after survey shows that privacy is a central concern for people who use the Internet. Consider the following:

- Sixty-two percent of respondents to a 2001 survey of Internet users by the Pew Internet & American Life Project wanted legislation to protect online privacy.

- Nearly two-thirds of respondents to a 2000 UCLA study felt that people who venture online put their privacy at risk.

- Sixty percent of Americans are particularly concerned about their personal information being included on electronic databases, according to research carried out by Gallup in 2000.

- In 2000, 79 percent of respondents to an American Express 2000 survey of consumer views towards online shopping were concerned about security and privacy when making an online transaction.

On the Internet everyone is a publisher and everyone has the opportunity to set up a website. What this means is that there are a lot of undesirables operating. Even respected organizations have shown a lax attitude to the collection and use of personal information about their customers and readers.

People are wary of giving away personal information. They are increasingly concerned about websites that collect information on them without their knowledge. Readers are therefore taking a very negative view of websites they feel are in any way abusing their privacy rights.

Reader privacy is a particularly important issue when it comes to establishing a subscription-based publication, or where a personalization system is being implemented. There are three basic principles that need to be employed when you are collecting personal information about readers:

- Inform them of any information you are collecting on them.

- Inform them what use you intend to make of this information.

- Allow them the right to view and delete information that has been collected on them.

Always be up-front with readers with regard to collecting personal information. Explain clearly the benefits they will receive as a result of giving you such details, and let them be the judge.

CONCLUSION

Realizing that the reader is king of the Web, and that everything about your website needs to be done with the reader in mind, is the key to online success. If you know your readers, know how they behave in our information-literate society, and know the seven things they want from your website, you'll be well on your way to success. Remember, the best word that sums up the online reader is – impatient.

References

Kathleen Anton, "Effective Intranet Publishing: Getting Critical Knowledge to Any Employee, Anywhere," *Intranet Design Magazine*, January 4, 2001

Steve Barth, "The Power of One," Knowledge Management Magazine, December 2000

Julie B. Morrison, Peter Pirolli and Stuart K. Card, "A taxonomic analysis of what World Wide Web activities significantly impact people's decisions and actions," Xerox Palo Alto Research Center, April 2001

Jakob Nielsen, *Designing Web Usability: the practice of simplicity*, New Riders, 2000

THE NEED FOR CONTENT STANDARDS

4

THE INTERNET: A TRIUMPH FOR STANDARDS

The development of the Internet is a triumph of common standards. There were computer networks before the Internet, but they were almost exclusively the same make of computer connected together. What the Internet achieved was to create a common standard whereby every computer in the world had the potential to be connected to a global network.

In 1968, J.C.R. Licklider and Robert Taylor espoused the need for common standards with regard to what would become the Internet when they wrote, "Creative, interactive communication requires a plastic or moldable medium that can be modeled, a dynamic medium in which premises will flow into consequences, and above all a common medium that can be contributed to and experimented with by all."

If the Internet was a triumph of common standards, the World Wide Web was equally so. Tim Berners-Lee, inventor of the Web, explaining its logic, wrote, "Despite the fact that numerous types of computers are used on the Web, and the fact that many of these machines are otherwise incompatible, those who 'publish' information on the Web are able to communicate with those who seek to access information with little difficulty because of these basic technical standards."

A good example of what happens when you don't have common standards within an information system is the 2000 American presidential election. Lack of common standards with regard to how votes were counted brought America to the verge of a constitutional crisis. The system had been crumbling for years. A tight race brought its flaws into sharp focus. A great many other information systems are also in tatters. It is only a matter of time before their flaws are exposed.

THE INTERNET TODAY IS A MESS

A customer walks into your reception area. They are hit with a pungent, acrid smell. As their nose twitches, they walk hesitantly to the counter. Their watering eyes are pulled to a bowl of fruit. The fruit is months old, soggy, withered and stinking. Feeling nauseous and disgusted, the customer leaves your office as quickly as possible.

Every day customers are leaving websites, turned off by out-of-date, poor-quality content. People would never leave bowls of stinking fruit in their reception areas, yet too many constantly leave out-of-date content on their websites. A 2000 survey by NOP of large UK firms found that 77 percent admitted their websites contained out-of-date content.

When Giga Information Group launched its website certification program in 2000, it stated that, "Giga's research has found that most websites fail to meet minimum standards" and that "we are astounded by the number of websites that look great but don't provide basic information and functionality for visitors." Have you ever wanted to find contact information on an organization on a website? Have you ever found that for this most simple and basic piece of content you have had to spend far too long searching? Join the club.

The future of the Internet and the Web must be about content standards, because if it isn't the Internet will collapse under the weight of information overload.

The future of the Internet and the Web must be about content standards, because if it isn't the Internet will collapse under the weight of information overload. While the current Web standard (HTML – Hyper Text Mark-up Language) deals with how content is laid out on a screen, future standards must deal with how content is created, edited, published and searched.

The current lack of standards contributes to a situation where:

- poor quality content is being created;
- content is not being properly organized and classified which makes the right content much more difficult to find;
- content is not being properly presented, making it difficult to read;
- content is moving too slowly through the editorial process and not getting published on time;
- a lack of review processes means that large quantities of out-of-date and inaccurate content is building up on the Web;

- organizations are faced with a proliferation of websites with no consistent standards for quality or presentation;
- money is being lost through dissatisfied readers (customers, staff) and inefficient publishing processes.

THE THIRD PHASE OF THE INTERNET

If the invention of the Internet was the first phase, and the invention of the Web was the second, then, as Bill Gates put it, "XML is the third phase of the Internet." XML (Extensible Mark-up Language) in itself is not important. It's the thinking behind XML that's important. XML is a form of metadata (which we will examine in more detail in Chapter 7). XML is about creating commonly-agreed standards for how content is classified and structured. XML is not some magic wand. Rather, it is a framework that facilitates the creation of common standards for content.

HTML was the original standard for presentation of text-based content on the Web, whereas XML is a standard for the "structuring" of content. XML tries to get everyone in a particular content area to agree that they will create the same "table of contents" structure for their content. It tries to get everyone to create content using similar processes.

In the financial industry, for example, that would mean the "morning notes" that analysts at financial institutions write (these are short documents published on a daily basis, describing the performance of a stock) would have the same layout and structure, and would use the same terms to describe their content.

This sounds complicated but it's not really. Let's say all the financial institutions, such as Bear Stearns, Morgan Stanley or Goldman Sachs agree that they will publish their research using a common XML standard. Let's look at the example of a morning note. Let's say that the financial institutions agree to use the same generic morning note template structure.

This template might begin with a heading field, then a summary field, followed by an author field, a body-text field, a ticker symbol field and a "buy, sell or hold" field. With the financial institutions inputting their content in the same type of template, the reader (fund manager) is given a huge degree of flexibility with regard to how they can search for the exact content they need. They could quickly design a system whereby they get a title and summary on 10 specified stocks from 15 specified financial institutions. They could set up a table that would track the "buy, sell or hold" statements of various financial institutions over a period of time.

XML gets deep into the content to provide a common standard with regard to how the content is organized. With 550 billion documents on the Internet and more appearing all the time, a common standard such as XML for how content is organized is not just an attractive option. It is essential.

However, because it is essential does not mean it will happen in every case it should. While many entities, such as the UN Center for Trade Facilitation and OASIS – a consortium of high-tech giants including IBM, Sun Microsystems and Hewlett-Packard – are embracing XML, there are already some troubling signs. According to TechWeb, "the proliferation of industry-specific XML dialects may create more confusion than communication as IT managers try to build B2B systems."

XML allows you to create a standard for how content is organized. That doesn't ultimately mean that a proper standard will be developed, or that it will be adhered to. The alternative, of course, is information overload.

STANDARDS EMPOWER

An unfortunate ideology took root in the early days of the Web. It was a kind of technological libertarianism, where individuals' rights to do just exactly as they pleased was seen as an unquestionable tenet of the new medium. This libertarianism mixed with the proclivities of traditional designers, whose instincts told them that if the Web was invented after MTV then it must be an extension of MTV. To add more spice to a turgid mixture, you had programmers who felt the Web was a playground for new technologies.

In the first couple of years of the Web the very idea that it should become commercial was anathema to a great many of the pioneers. While this view quickly disappeared, a tendency toward

> **Again and again, you will find designers and programmers who want to express themselves first and serve the reader second.**

extreme individualism still results in a great many websites being poorly designed. Again and again, you will find designers and programmers who want to express themselves first and serve the reader second. This is not good business, and these people need to take a back seat.

Ultimately, it is not good design practice either, because the true beauty in a design rests first and foremost in its usefulness. When we think of great design, the Apple Mac comes to mind. The Mac's beauty was in its elegance and simplicity. The Volkswagen Beetle is also regarded as a classic design. However, first and foremost it was a robust, dependable and affordable car. Bang & Olufsen makes classic hi-fi equipment that is known for its technical brilliance but functional simplicity. Great designers strive for a simplicity of function and an elegance of style.

The Web is fundamentally a text-driven medium. When it comes to text, the originality of style is in the words, not in the graphics. The fundamentals of Web design are driven not by how the page looks but rather by how it reads. The fundamentals of Web design deal with how the content is created and presented. What matters is how easy it is for a reader to read content, how the reader can navigate the classification system, how they can search for a particular document, how easy it is for them to move back and forth through the website.

All of these fundamentals beg for a common-standards approach. We're not talking just about an XML common standard, but rather common standards with regard to how the entire website is designed and managed.

We need to get something crystal clear here. A common standard empowers rather than restricts the writer, editor and reader. A common standard for the publication of the website allows them to focus on what's really important – the content. Unfortunately, again and again, those who are charged with managing a website have focussed on the wrong sort of design. They resist common standards, claiming that the Web is about freedom, when it is actually the result of a common standard.

Ulysses by James Joyce and *The Brothers Karamazov* by Fyodor Dostoyevsky are regarded as classics of literature. Is this because of the font type and size they use? The way they lay out the text, perhaps? The dimensions of the books? The chapter structure? Perhaps it's because of the innovative color coding of Ulysses, whereby every page is a different shade of green? Or perhaps it's how in Dostoyevsky's book the print is a fluorescent yellow that glows in the dark so you don't require a light to read it? Or maybe it's because of the ideas, the plots and the style used in the writing?

Spread out the world's 100 bestselling English-language newspapers and you will find only a few types of layouts. There will be only two basic sizes – tabloid and broadsheet. The front pages of the broadsheets will be laid out in a very similar way. The name of the newspaper will be at the top, for example. There will generally be only five to seven stories on the page, with the lead story given prominence at the top of the page. Often there will be a large photograph with this story. Text will be presented in short paragraphs. If there are ads, they will be across the bottom of the page or in the bottom right-hand corner.

The reason for all this uniformity of layout style is that over time newspapers have found that there are defined ways to present content that allow the reader to absorb it in the easiest and most efficient way. Having a uniform layout does not make newspapers uniform. They differentiate themselves by their choice of content, by what they consider to be important content, and by the tone in which they write it.

Having a common standard for the way you present your content on the Web does not make your website uniform. What it does is to provide the reader with an efficient way of looking at it. What makes you unique or standard or dull or exciting is not the visual design of your website. Studies have shown that a large number of people who regularly use the Web go straight for the text, ignoring the graphics entirely. Two things make you different and successful in a text-driven environment:

- The ability of the reader to get to the content they need as quickly and easily as possible.
- The quality and presentation of that content.

For managers, a common standard for content allows them to "manage." A great many websites today have become unmanageable because of their chaotic nature. A common standard gives power back to managers to do the job they're employed to do. It also delivers more than just the ability to manage – it allows managers to carry out their job efficiently and cost-effectively. Chaotic environments waste an incredible amount of time, energy and money. By their very nature they are almost impossible to plan for.

A website publication built around common standards saves time and delivers much better results, and, just as important, it can evolve logically. On a chaotic website you find a common pattern occurring every twelve months or so. It's called "trash and build again." This approach comes from a lack of planning and common standards. With good planning and common standards you can revamp your website, add a new section, etc., in an efficient and cost-effective way. It'll save you time and money. And your reader will be much happier with the result.

FIGURE 4.1

What is striking about the layout and design of these four newspapers is how similar they are. Nearly all broadsheet newspapers follow the same basic layout approach.

The Web has often been described as a library with all the books on the floor and the lights turned out. What is a library? A library is a place where readers can find books because they are organized in a logical manner. While every library will have a different collection of books, the vast majority of public and commercial libraries use a common classification approach.

Classification sounds like something technical, something that managers should leave to somebody else to do. Wrong. Next to the quality of your content, classification is the most important thing a website requires. Classification is the expression of strategy in its most distilled and precise manner.

Are you selling "products," "services" or "solutions"? Do you have a product offering targeted at "large corporations" and "small and medium enterprises"? These are strategic questions. They are also classification questions. Basically, if senior management is not intimately involved in guiding the development of the classification of its websites, those websites are less likely to reflect the strategic focus of the organization. If they do not reflect this strategic focus, then what exactly are they for?

A common approach to classification is fundamental to the success of any Internet strategy. While we will deal with classification in greater detail in later chapters, it is important to note that classification is being seen by an increasing number of organizations as a priority in Web design. For example:

- As of July 2000, Merrill Lynch had about 200 registered intranet sites, representing a 40 percent growth on the year previously. One way Merrill Lynch is responding to an increasingly chaotic content environment is to establish common classification systems.

- Hershey Foods Corporation has initiated a classification program with the objective of naming "categories the way folks would look for information," according to Joni Pfautz, Internet/intranet co-ordinator at Hershey.

- Intel has more than one million URLs on its intranet, with more than 100 new websites introduced every month. "Categorization [classification] of corporate information is critical because it provides employees with a navigation directory that can be browsed to find specific information," an Intel white paper stated in 2001.

- Wal-Mart had 36 departments because in the early days its NCR cash registers came with only 36 keys. When it applied this classification structure to the Web, the result was that sunglasses were listed in the automotive department. Realizing that sales online would be hurt without proper classification, Wal-Mart.com redesigned the structure. Now you can find sunglasses classified with suntan lotion, rather than with brake fluid.

STANDARDS ALLOW MORE PEOPLE TO PUBLISH

Content standards allow more people with fewer technical or design skills to become active participants in the publishing process. It is often the people who need to participate – authors and editors – who don't have such skills.

It is almost unimaginable that in today's economy someone will progress to the highest levels within a modern organization without top-notch publishing skills.

Imagine if in an organization of 1,000 staff only one person could type. Think of the bottleneck that would exist. Hundreds of people would want to create content but they would have to write by hand and then give these written documents to the busy typist. Such an organization would not last long.

Twenty years ago, very few managers typed. An army of typists supported a battalion of managers. Today, any manager who can't type (at least with two fingers!) is either over sixty or has no ambition. It is almost unimaginable that in today's economy someone will progress to the highest levels within a modern organization without top-notch publishing skills.

Today, a major bottleneck in getting content published on the Web is the fact that authors and editors are often highly dependent on technical resources (HTML or programing) to get their content published or to make any sort of layout changes to the Website. In an environment where time-to-publish is becoming even more critical, this is costly and counter-productive.

According to Tenopir and King (1997), the fixed cost of a "first copy" of a quality document in academic publishing can be as high as $4,000. Because academic salaries tend to be lower than those within many commercial environments, the first-copy cost of a commercial report may in fact be higher. A way to reduce these costs is to spread publishing skills as widely through the organization as possible.

In academia this is already happening. Odlyzko (1997) states that, "Most scholars are already typesetting their own papers. Many were forced to do so by cutbacks in secretarial support. However, even among those, there are few who would go back to the old system of depending on technical typists if they had a choice. Technology is making it easier to do many tasks oneself than to explain to others how to do them. Editors and referees are increasingly processing electronic submissions, even for journals that appear exclusively in print. Moreover, the general consensus is that this makes their life much easier."

Varian (1997) states that, "If all articles were submitted and distributed electronically, I would guess that the costs of the editorial process would drop by a factor of 50 percent due to the reduction in clerical labor costs, postage, photocopying, etc."

The benefits of spreading an organization's publishing skills include:

- People are more empowered with regard to the content they create.
- Administrative costs are reduced and the whole publishing process is more streamlined.
- Bottlenecks are greatly diminished, therefore reducing the time it takes to get a particular document published.

The Web is inherently a distributed publishing medium. Unfortunately, we have seen that distributed publishing without commonly-agreed standards results in chaos. This book will help you develop a strategy whereby you can fully tap into the ability of every worker in the organization to create relevant content, while at the same time making sure that the strategy is built around common standards so that the environment can be managed in a cost-effective and professional manner.

A classic problem, particularly within intranet design, is whether to have one central website with various sections, or to have many individual websites loosely linked together. (This problem applies only to large organizations.) In reality, the question is somewhat redundant if you take a standards-based approach to content.

In 2000, Larry Ellison, chief executive of Oracle, spoke about how the company saved $1 billion by standardizing the way it managed its intranets. He talked about how Oracle had previously essentially lost control of its component parts. He mentioned as an example the fact that the French division of Oracle had taken it upon itself to design its own Oracle logo.

The bottom line is that, as in every other area of business, standards and policies are necessary for the efficient and cost-effective functioning of a website. Without direction from the center, you get mini-websites that take on a life of their own and essentially become independent entities. This will hurt an organization's cohesion, and will mean that the website's ability to communicate core organizational strategy and culture will be severely weakened.

It is true that standards can go too far and be too rigid. This will make people feel constrained and restricted. It is imperative that the essential "rules of the road" are agreed throughout the organization with regard to how publishing design will be approached. Once these rules are in place, there can be flexibility on customizing designs for particular departments, regions or product groups. Of course, a much greater degree of control can be given with regard to the type of content to be published, so that it can accurately reflect the needs and culture of that particular department or marketplace.

Central standards save everyone time and trouble. An analogy can be made to the libraries in any particular country. They will all have a different selection of books, but will all invariably use a common library classification system for organizing the books on their shelves.

Common standards are by no means an end in themselves. It will always be content that will make a website original and useful. It will be people that will create, edit and publish this content. In the following chapters we will examine the key processes involved in publishing quality content cost-effectively. We have broken these processes up into three key groups – creation, editing and publishing – within which there are a number of supporting processes. The idea is to take the mystery out of publishing – to examine it in a logical and concise way.

Not every publishing process will be relevant to every organization. However, an in-depth understanding of how quality publishing works is necessary if you want to get the right content to the right person at the right time – and at the right cost.

Above all, as you read through what follows, remember that publishing is at heart a people business. At every step of that way, those who are expected to create, edit and publish need to be fully engaged. There are many organizations with content management systems that are impressive technological structures but little more than empty shells or, even worse, content dumps, behind their facades.

References

Tim Berners-Lee, "Information Management: A Proposal" (This is the original proposal for the World Wide Web.) CERN, March 1989. http://www.w3.org/History/1989/proposal.html

Bill Gates, "XML: third phase of the Internet," speech, Enterprise Solutions Conference, Miami, March 2000

J.C.R. Licklider, "Man-Computer Symbiosis," *IRE Transactions on Human Factors in Electronics*, Volume HFE-1, March 1960

J.C.R. Licklider and Robert Taylor, "The Computer as a Communication Device," *Science and Technology*, April 1968

Andrew Odlyzko, *The Economics of Electronic Journals*, First Monday, August 1997

Carol Tenopir and Donald W. King, "Trends in Scientific Scholarly Journal Publishing in the United States," *Journal of Scholarly Publishing*, April 1997

Hal R. Varian, *The Evolution of Journals: The Future of Electronic Journals*, University of California, Berkeley, 1997. http://www.press.umich.edu/jep/04-01/varian.html

CREATING CONTENT

5

The following three chapters examine the processes of creating, editing and publishing content. In this chapter we look at content creation. You need to make two kinds of analyses before you begin creating or adding content. The first is to identify your readers – making sure you understand the desires and needs of the existing and potential readers of your website. The second is to identify your content – both reviewing your website's current content and considering what else you should add to satisfy readers and further your organizational objectives.

Once you've identified your readers and your content needs, there are a number of strategies you can pursue to generate this content. You can create it fresh from within your organization or you can acquire it from a third party. Another alternative – one that's almost unique to the Web – is to get your readers to become active in creating content.

IDENTIFYING YOUR READERS

Readers are the people who buy your products and services (customers), work for your organization (staff), think of working for you (potential staff), invest in your organization (investors), write about your organization in the press (journalists) – in other words, anyone with an interest or a potential interest in your organization. People come to the Web primarily to read. People come to your website primarily to read. Before you consider anything else you've got to understand the nature of your target reader.

Understanding your reader is a vital first step in ensuring that the Internet becomes a vehicle through which you successfully implement your objectives and strategies. Your readers can have a direct impact on your business, either positive (buying items from you, or investing in your company), or negative (complaining about you to others, writing a critical article about you). The importance of a particular type of reader will depend on their potential impact on your business.

(In identifying your reader, you should expect some crossover with the process of identifying content for that reader. However, we are treating them as separate tasks, since they involve a number of different steps.)

How many types of readers?

The characteristics of your readers will also affect the type of content you provide and the format in which you present it. If you are managing an intranet, for example, the target reader seems simple. It's your staff. But it's *not* that simple. Is it the entire staff, or are there certain departments that have a more pressing need for content than others? If you have a large sales-force out on the road, perhaps they should be the primary readers? Do the product development people have a critical need for up-to-date content?

Most websites will have more than one type of target reader. Readers from different regions (US, Germany, etc.) may prefer content to be classified together for their particular region. Readers who are interested in a particular product will want all the content connected with that product to be classified together. In an intranet environment, readers who want human resource information will prefer to see it all classified together.

Don't try to cater to all

While the Web is by definition an international medium, its global reach should not be overplayed. You may well end up having readers from 50 countries, but that doesn't mean you should shape your publication for each of those countries. A website that attempts to tailor itself for too many target readers is likely to end up satisfying nobody's needs. The bottom line is whether it makes economic sense to target a particular type of reader.

A lot of the thinking that drove Web publications in the early days was to get as many readers as possible. This approach makes sense for the small number of websites whose readers are paying a subscription fee. Otherwise, you need to focus on the quality of the reader rather than the quantity. If you have an e-commerce site, for instance, it's better to have 100 readers per day leading to 10 sales, than 1,000 casual readers who produce no sales.

The Web is a fluid, evolving medium. When you launch, expand or redesign your website, you may find that you are getting a new type of reader, that you've opened up a new market segment. If that happens, you must be able to further adapt the content for this new reader.

Get everyone on board

In deciding who the readers are and prioritizing them, it is essential that you get "buy-in" from all the key constituencies in the organization. If this doesn't happen, what will invariably occur is that a key reader will be missed, or will be prioritized incorrectly. What is also likely to happen is that later in the process when content and participation are required, you will not get sufficient co-operation.

If your Web strategy is simple, you may feel you've already adequately identified your readers. Perhaps you've done all the analysis you need to do as you've read the first few pages of this chapter. But if your strategy is more complex, or if you want to conduct a more formal review of your website, you may find it useful to work through the following checklist.

Checklist: identify the reader

Analyze:

- Current website – if there is one, find out as much as possible about who is visiting it. Get feedback internally about who are seen as target readers.
- Competitors' websites – check out your major competitors and try to see what sort of readers they are targeting.
- Industry websites – have a look at the leading industry websites to see what type of readers they are pitched at.

Consult:

- Meet key constituents in your organization in one-to-one meetings or in a workshop environment, sharing and discussing findings from the analysis. Key constituents are people or departments responsible for supplying critical content to the website, probably on an ongoing basis. If you do not consult them about identifying the reader, it will be more difficult to secure their co-operation in supplying you with the content you need.

Survey:

- Depending on the size of the proposed publication, the budget and the time constraints, you may want to interview a few readers or conduct a more formal survey of a larger group. Whatever approach you take, you will want answers to the following types of questions:

- What is the most critical content that your reader requires?
- What critical content are they not getting?
- How do they like to consume their content?
- How do they like it presented?
- What sort of publications are they using to receive their content?
- Do they view you as a legitimate source for content?

Prioritize:

■ Draw up a list of all potential readers.

■ Hold workshops with the key constituents to prioritize this list. Give each reader on it a priority rating from 1 to 10. It may be that you will end up with a group of primary and secondary readers. The emphasis of the publication will be on the primary readers, but content will be available for secondary readers too.

Obtain sign-off:

■ This is vital. If you can't get sign-off on your readers, then all the other processes become, to some degree, invalid. Generating content for the wrong reader is a costly process. Furthermore, presenting the wrong content on the website is likely to confuse and alienate the reader you need to reach.

IDENTIFYING YOUR CONTENT

Once you have identified your target readers, you are ready to identify the content you need to deliver to further the organization's objectives and strategies. In an ideal world you would identify lots of high-quality content to deliver to the reader. However, quality content is expensive and we must accept that there will be a trade-off between the ultimate content and the cost of generating it on an ongoing basis.

Content is critical. It is the lifeblood of the vast majority of websites. Get the reader wrong and you're wasting your time. Get the content wrong for the reader and you're wasting both your time and theirs!

What have you got?

What content is up on your website? What, if any, is the gap between the amount of content the reader needs and the amount of content that the organization is generating? What, if any, is the gap in the quality of content between what the reader expects and what the organization is delivering? Is the content being published on time? Is published content out of date? Is the reader getting information from the organization that is wrong or misleading?

What is the gap in the quality of content between what the reader expects and what the organization is delivering? Is the content being published on time? Is published content out of date?

What other potentially useful content is there within the organization? What sort of content do competitors have on their websites, or in other publication mediums? What sort of relevant content is being published by the industry, government, etc.? Obviously, the length you will go to in this sort of analysis will depend on the type of publication you are creating. If, for example, it is an intranet publication, the amount of analysis will be less than for a public website.

What language?

The language or set of languages in which the website is to be published needs to be addressed. Even if English is the only language to be used, is it American English or British English? Again, the target reader will have a central influence here. If it's predominantly a British audience, then logic would dictate that it should be British English. However, this may create some confusion for Americans and other non-British readers.

Language can be a particularly sensitive area. You may need to have more than one language for political, rather than economic, reasons. By no means everyone on the Web wants to read English. (In France, there's a law against it!) Research published by the Aberdeen Group in May 2001 predicted that by 2003, "66 percent of all e-commerce spending will originate outside the US." The report went on to state that, "if a product or website is not optimized for international transactions, the logistics of marketing to an international market can be crippling, with return rates as high as 46 percent for all products sold internationally." People stay twice as long on sites that have content in their own language, and are four times more likely to buy something from a native language website, the report found.

A second language will not double the cost of the publication, but it will add significantly to it. Over time, having a second language can be a lot like having a second publication, as websites in different languages tend to evolve differently. A German website, for example, will require different content to a website in English, as it is targeted at different markets and cultures. It is likely that as these sites grow, dedicated publishing teams will be required to run them. These teams will probably be best located in the country of the particular language, as this will allow them better to understand the specific content required.

Scoping your website

The organization needs to establish the basic scope of the publication to get an idea of the amount of content it needs to deliver to meet its readers' needs and further its own objectives. While a certain amount of content will be obvious, you will never get it exactly right the first time. It is therefore essential to be willing to adapt and change, dropping the content that isn't working, expanding the content that is, and introducing new content classifications where needed.

The publication scope will be significantly influenced by the budget. It will be easy to list a whole range of preferred content from talking to the key constituents. However, quality content is expensive, and you will inevitably find that having so much content is simply not economic. You first need to establish the "must-have" content for the website; the content that the website requires to meet the essential needs of its readers. In an intranet, an example might be information on meeting-room availability. If staff can find out which rooms are booked and which are available, they will want to visit the intranet regularly.

Will you also want to deliver some of your website's content via subscription-based publishing (email), personalization systems, mobile phones, interactive TV, third-party media, print, etc.? (Chapter 10 covers subscription-based publishing in more detail.) Choosing additional media for delivering your content will depend on your target readers and the way they want the content delivered. But it's important to understand that choosing extra publication mediums for your content can greatly add to the complexity and cost of the project. Be careful not to assume that content generated for the Web will immediately transfer to other media. For example, mobile phone content will probably have to be written much more concisely.

Pick a publication schedule

How frequently will the website be updated? Daily? Weekly? The publication schedule you choose has a major impact on the scope and cost of your website. Remember that the more frequent the publication schedule, the more costly the publication will be. Again, a key factor will be the expectation and needs of the reader.

You will need to work out how much content will be published on the website on a daily, weekly or monthly basis, and what elements of the publication will remain relatively fixed from a content perspective. For example, content for "product features" will not change as often as a "what's new" feature. How often will the homepage be changed? It needs to be agreed whether this will be once a day (and at what time), once a week, or whatever. Subsidiary homepages may be changed less frequently.

Once a publication schedule has been established, it must be rigidly adhered to. If the homepage is to be "published" at 10am every weekday, then your readers will *expect* it to be updated at 10am on the dot every weekday. If you buy a newspaper each morning, what's your reaction if it's not there at the regular time? If that keeps happening you'll likely stop reading that paper. Web readers expect information to be up to date. If they get used to checking your website at certain times for new content and that new content is not there, they will stop visiting.

The publication schedule should also stipulate the times when there will be no new content published, for example on public holidays, at Christmas and so on. The website should tell its readers the dates.

Content forms and types

A key step in identifying content is to pinpoint the various content forms and types. You need to know roughly what percentage of total content is in the form of text, audio and video, and what percentage is interactive. For most websites, the vast majority of content is text. Remember that audio and video tend to be more expensive to create than text, and that neither audio nor video is nearly as well suited as text to the current Web.

In relation to a particular content form, what are the discrete content types? For example, in relation to text, there could be event content, general article content, customer profile, procedure and policy, staff human resources and so on. Each discrete type will require its own document template.

Interactive content may come in the form of bookable meeting-room calendars, searchable staff databases and so on.

Cost-benefit analysis

It's easy to get carried away in identifying content and end up with a massive publication that is hugely expensive to produce. Unless your business model involves charging the reader directly for your content, it is often difficult to quantify the exact return that content delivers. However, that does not mean that you should not apply as rigorous a cost benefit analysis as possible. Ultimately, every item of content created should deliver either a direct or indirect benefit. Otherwise, it should not be published on your website. (Content cost-benefit analysis is dealt with in Chapter 2.)

Checklist: identifying content

Analyze:

- Take an inventory of the content on your website, and of content available in other media within the organization.
- Compare what you have with the results of your analysis of your readers, and identify gaps.
- Draw up a report detailing the salient points. Make sure the key constituents in the organization get copies.

Agree:

- Identify the language approach. Identify key cost implications of additional languages.

- Decide on the publication medium. As well as the Web, will it be email, WAP, print, etc.? Flag integration issues and their associated costs. Get sign-off.

- Agree, at least at a high level, on the publication schedule. It's not essential to get a final sign-off here, though it is important to get a good fix on how much new content will be published on the website in any particular period.

- Define publication scope. Define "must-have" versus "like-to-have" content. A detailed list should be compiled. The scope may evolve, but you should strive to get sign-off on the "must have" content as soon as possible.

Identify:

- Isolate the forms of content that need to be created – text-based, audio, video, interactive.

- Identify the content types within each form.

Establish a cost-benefit framework:

- What are the key benefits that the publication will provide?

- What are the key costs? (See Chapter 2.)

CREATING CONTENT: CRITICAL FACTORS

Once you have identified the type of content you require for your reader, the next step is to examine how that content can be best created. Traditionally, an author creates content as a result of a request from an editor. There are situations where content is unsolicited, but this tends to be more the exception than the rule. It goes without saying that all content created should reflect the publication scope, as defined in the previous section.

There needs to be a broad policy on the creation approach. Will it be largely single-author, or will collaborative authoring be encouraged? The approach will have an impact on the creation tools. In some cases, the content will be created directly through the content management application. However, in most cases, some sort of word processing or other software package will be used first. Whatever the general approach, the organization should strive to standardize the tools being used, as this will make the whole operation more manageable and cost-effective.

In most environments there will be large amounts of content already created by the organization. For cost and time reasons, it may not be practical for the organization to rewrite all of it specifically for the Web. Therefore a technical approach may be required to convert, for example, Excel spreadsheets into a Web-based table layout.

Style and readability guidelines

Without a common policy on style and tone, the website will become disjointed and difficult to read. It will give the impression that the organization is not cohesive, that it does not have a professional approach to delivering its message. Style and tone guidelines should also deal with key spelling and grammar. Spelling should be uniform, not "e-commerce" in one document and "ecommerce" in another. In addition to the organization's internal style guide, an independently published style guide should be designated (*The Web Content Style Guide*, by McGovern, Norton and O'Dowd, is the most comprehensive and authoritative style guide for online writers). A website should also choose a default dictionary to help writers and editors decide minor variations in spelling and usage.

Closely associated with style is what might be termed the "readability" of the content. In an age where complexity is rampant and people are busy and confused, we strongly recommend a simple, direct style for the Web. To make your content as readable as possible, consider the following guidelines when creating content:

- Write simply and clearly.
- Write for your reader, not for your ego.
- Keep sentences, paragraphs and documents short. Sentences should be between 10 and 15 words. Paragraphs should average about 50 words

at most. The optimal length for a Web document is between 500 and 700 words. Remember, we live in an age of attention-deficit – readers will not read long documents unless they have a very good reason.

FIGURE 5.1

MIDEAST STRUGGLE FOR PEACE

Issues | Key Players | Maps | Timeline | Landscapes | People of Israel | Quiz | Overview
Key Documents | Related Sites | Message Board | Video Archive

U.S. urges peace as bombs rattle Jerusalem

May 27, 2001 Posted: 3:18 p.m. EDT (1918 GMT)

(AP PHOTO)

More than 20 were treated for shock and injuries sustained in the blasts

JERUSALEM (CNN) -- Against a backdrop of continuing violence in Jerusalem, senior U.S. diplomat William Burns met Sunday with Israeli Prime Minister Ariel Sharon and his foreign and defense ministers.

Burns said he and Sharon discussed ways of implementing the Mitchell Report, named after former U.S. Sen. George Mitchell, which calls for an immediate, unconditional cease-fire followed by a cooling-off period, confidence-building measures and a resumption of peace negotiations.

Burns told Sharon he appreciated Israel's policy of restraint in the face of continuing violence.

But Sharon responded that Israel cannot continue to adhere to that policy indefinitely, according to a statement released by his office. He reiterated his view that violence must stop before peace talks can resume.

Israeli Foreign Minister Shimon Peres said it is important for both sides to follow the sequence of events laid out in the report.

But the Palestinians have said they want to speed things up and get back to peace talks as soon as possible.

This CNN story, with lots of links, and short, punchy paragraphs, is designed specifically for the Web so that a "scan reader" can digest it quickly.

- Write punchy, no-nonsense headings.

- Write short, clear summaries that answer, if possible, the where, when, what and why.

- You may choose to have your website in English only, but still want to reach an international English-speaking audience. Therefore you must avoid colloquialisms and jargon. Clear, simple, precise and unambiguous English should be used.

Word and phrase glossary

It is important to achieve a "common language" understanding within the organization. Words and phrases must mean the same thing to all authors, otherwise the message becomes confused and the reader becomes confused. A way of establishing a common language approach is to have a keyword and phrase glossary, which defines key terms and how they are spelled. Everyone who is creating content must then adhere to this glossary.

A word and phrase glossary should be laid out as follows:

- Present first the top 20/30 critical words and phrases about which there needs to be a common understanding within the organization.

- In an A-Z format, present the entire list of words and phrases commonly used when content is created for the organization.

- Avoid having too long a list.

Content layout

The way the content is to be laid out may have implications for the creation process. When creating content, authors need to be aware of and adhere to content layout standards that have a direct impact on the creation process.

An example of how content layout would affect an author would be the way in which long documents are dealt with. Such documents require tables of contents for optimal readability on the Web. Obviously if the author does not include sub-headings in their document, then these tables of contents cannot be easily created. Content layout issues are dealt with in detail in Chapter 9, but the implications, where appropriate, should be fed back into the creation process.

Creating content collaboratively

There is a romantic image of writers as solitary figures toiling away in an attic for years and finally emerging with a masterpiece. This is simply not the case in business or academia.

There is a romantic image of writers as solitary figures toiling away in an attic for years, and finally emerging with a masterpiece. While this may still be true for fiction writers – though even Shakespeare collaborated – it is simply not the case in business or academia. In both sectors, writing is an increasingly collaborative activity.

The reason why collaborative writing is increasing and will become even more common is simple. Much of our writing now exists within a digital networked medium. The tool has always had a huge influence on how humans do things, and as the tools of writing change so too will the form and shape of writing.

Specifically, there are a number of factors driving collaborative writing:

- Replicability – digital content is easy, cheap and fast to copy. Each copy is a perfect copy. The result is that many people can work on the same content.

- Common medium – the Internet is a common medium that allows for fast, cheap and ongoing communication over long distances.

- Common tools – authors have the same or similar software tools (word processing, email, etc.) which allow them to work collaboratively more easily.

- Changeability – digital documents are easy to change, add notes to, etc.

- Compactness – digital documents, particularly text-based ones, are relatively small and can therefore be moved quickly and efficiently between authors.

- Hypertext – hypertext is changing the whole way we write content. Documents are getting shorter and more interlinked. This invites collaboration.

- Information overload – not only is the amount of content exploding, the information contained in content is changing with increasing frequency. Collaboration allows people to pool resources and keep up with rapidly changing trends.

It is not surprising that the Internet has become a hotbed of collaboration, as that was one of the primary motivations for its invention. J.C.R. Licklider was perhaps the key inspiration behind the Internet. His vision of the computer was not as a computational device, but rather as a communications tool. In the late Sixties he wrote that, "Its presence can change the nature and value of communication even more profoundly than did the printing press and the picture tube, for, as we shall show, a well-programed computer can provide direct access both to informational resources and to the *processes* for making use of the resources." For Licklider, collaboration was one of the key processes that a networked computer would open up.

FIGURE 5.2

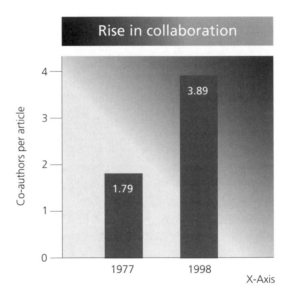

Source: D. King, ISI Science Citation Index

According to a 2000 report from The Yankee Group, which studied 200 companies and how they do business on the Internet, "The key to success in the long term is continued hands-on involvement by management and cross-functional teamwork between multiple organizational units." Cisco talks about the emergence of an "Internet ecosystem" where, "The open nature of the Internet encourages complementary business alliances that create a unique set of interwoven dependencies and relationships. Since

Internet ecosystems are open, they encourage new members to participate and foster a collaborative relationship among members."

Collaborative writing works best where:

- there is a major content creation task at hand that ideally demands the input of multiple disciplines;
- the content job can be broken up into clearly defined segments that can be allocated to individual authors. However, just allocating pieces of work to people is not collaboration. Unless there is strong interaction between authors, and an overall sense of direction and style is jointly established, you will not achieve the true potential of collaboration;
- there are tight publication deadlines, which means that a number of authors are more likely to deliver a quality result on time;
- there is a well thought-through set of processes to facilitate collaboration.

Collaboration is not easy

Collaboration is not easy because the classical business environment rewards individual effort. A great many people believe the motto "knowledge is power," with the logical extension that individual knowledge is individual power. It can also be the case that the better the writer the bigger the ego.

Add to this the fact that a lot of people who can easily accept criticism in other areas become very tetchy when their writing is criticized, and you can understand the difficulty in achieving quality collaboration. To top it all off, while obvious mistakes can be pointed out and accepted, two people may have very different but perfectly acceptable styles. Unfortunately, writing is an inexact science – more like a craft, really – and there is rarely one right way to write up a piece of content.

People will collaborate better if:

- they know each other and have a respect for the skills and knowledge each party brings to the task;
- there is a clear reward and remuneration structure that supports collaborative writing;
- management shows a real commitment to collaboratively-created content, and is actively willing to promote such an approach;

- there is a similarity of style and thinking between the authors, or different parties bring very different skills. For example, one person has a deep technical understanding but relatively poor writing skills, whereas another has excellent writing skills;
- there is a shared understanding of what needs to be achieved and of the processes involved in getting to the finished product;
- there is an equal level of commitment and enthusiasm.

Motivation and reward

A core objective of every creation process should be to create as much quality content as possible. It is hard to think of any better way to encourage this than by motivating and rewarding more highly authors who create quality content than authors who create poor content. This is a critical problem that many content-publishing projects face. Unfortunately, content creation is often seen as a secondary activity, something you have to do after the job is done – a necessary evil. Staff are often expected to "do the paperwork" in their own time and little credit or reward is given.

If a proper motivation and reward structure is not put in place, there is less likelihood of a publishing strategy succeeding. In fact it is quite likely to be doomed.

There is an increasing awareness that staff should be properly rewarded for creating quality content, although in practice this is still at an early stage.

- In 2000, the Gartner Group estimated that some 15 percent of its clients were financially rewarding their staff for contributing quality information to the organization.
- At IBM, anyone who creates content that another employee uses to win more than $20,000 worth of new business is allowed to share a $5,000 reward. The reward is split to encourage both the creation of better content and its use.
- The public relations firm Hill and Knowlton has a reward scheme for staff who contribute content and ideas that help it create better methodologies for client-based work.
- Staff at Harvard Pilgrim Health Care are given between $1,000 and $5,000 for creating content that makes the organization more efficient. Harvard Pilgrim believes that the scheme encourages employees to stay as they see that their knowledge is genuinely valued.

There are various ways you can motivate authors to create quality content and reward them for doing so, including:

- Making content-creation part of their job. Content doesn't grow on trees, and people will not create quality content consistently if they are not expected to. More Web initiatives fail because they ignore this basic fact than perhaps for any other reason.

- Paying them. No matter how much people love to work, they have to get paid. If you want great content that is well written so that it can be easily understood, you need to pay for it. In this way the worker who creates quality content gets paid more than the worker who doesn't.

- Massaging their egos. It's always nice to see your name under the lead article on a website. So if someone creates a great document, promote that person and their document.

- Advancing their careers. Make it clear that those who contribute quality content consistently will move up through the organization.

- Linking in with learning. If workers are aware that creating quality content is an essential skill, they are more likely to want to learn how to become better at it.

- Championing co-operation. To fully co-operate you need to be able to share content – to give as well as take. If you create quality content that others can discuss and add to, you become a valuable part of the team.

Copyright and legal issues

Copyright protects content. A copyright policy needs to address issues such as – who owns the copyright of the content created for the organization? Is it the author or is it the organization itself? The question of copyright may need to be handled slightly differently with regard to content created by a full-time member of staff than content created by a freelance author. A copyright policy must also address the syndication of content by the organization. Broadly, the areas copyright must address can be broken down into two main categories:

For authors:

- The policy will define the circumstances under which an author may use and quote from third-party content. It will explain the concept of "fair use" and will give a step-by-step procedure with regard to an author acquiring copyright permission from third parties. This copyright document should also clearly explain to the author where the copyright resides. If it resides with the organization, then a statement is necessary regarding to the sale of such content to third parties. Does the author receive any commission on such sales?

For the reader:

- This copyright policy statement should be accessible from a link in the footer section of every page on the website. It should clearly state the conditions under which the organization's content can be used by third parties, and the procedure by which a third party must undertake to acquire copyright permission. This copyright page should include the legal name of the company, group name if part of a group, reader agreement if any, and information on any company trademarks.

The legal policy needs to articulate clearly to authors:

- libel issues;
- accuracy and fact issues;
- special legal conditions – if, for example, the website is promoting alcohol, what are the legal implications? Remember, a website potentially reaches every jurisdiction in the world; what's legal in one country may not be legal in another;
- trademark issues. It is not advisable to include trademark symbols on a Web page. Instead a copyright notice such as "Copyright © 1995-2001 Example Company. All rights reserved" should appear in the footer information of every page and link to a separate page for legal information (including trademarks and copyrights);

Authors should be advised to:

- check and double-check their facts;
- avoid directly criticizing a person or company unless they are absolutely certain of the facts;
- make sure that they have copyright permission for any third-party material they are using;
- avoid plagiarism; the use and representation of the writings of another person or organization as one's own. The ability to "cut and paste" content makes plagiarism seductively easy on the Web. There should be

serious penalties for intentional plagiarism, and an awareness of the dangers of unintentional plagiarism. The best way to avoid unintentional plagiarism is to insist on a rigorous and formal fact-checking process.

One of the most important legal issues on the Internet today is privacy. The organization will require a very clear statement on how it collects information on its readers and what it does with that information.

One of the most important legal issues on the Internet today is privacy. The organization will require a very clear statement on how it collects information on its readers and what it does with that information.

All copyright, related legal issues, and any relevant rules for the use of the website should come together into what is called a "terms of use" statement that will clearly explain to the reader the terms under which they can use the website. A terms of use statement should cover some or all of the following:

■ Privacy.

■ Copyright.

■ Software download/use.

■ Trademarks.

■ Patents.

■ License and site-access.

■ Links to third-party websites.

■ Reader-generated content.

■ Copyright complaints procedure.

■ Risk of loss (where products are being sold from the website).

■ Product descriptions (where products are being sold).

■ Disclaimer of warranties and limitation of liability.

■ Contact information.

Checklist: creating and adapting content

- Decide on the content creation approach and tools. Establish what is the basic approach to creating content (individual, collaborative). Establish what type of software is being used.

- Flag content conversion issues.

- Establish whether there is already a style and tone guide within the organization. Choose a published style guide and common dictionary. Agree on style and tone issues. Get sign-off.

- Establish whether there is already a word and phrase glossary within the organization. Agree on an approach to creating one. Assign responsibility.

- Define and detail content layout issues that will have an impact on authors.

- Agree on policies for motivation and reward.

- Address all relevant copyright and legal issues. Create a table of contents for the terms of use, and assign responsibility. Legal expertise will be required here. Once policies have been developed, authors should be properly informed.

COMMISSIONING CONTENT

Content should be commissioned when the editor recognizes a need for a certain type of content that will be created only if it is actively sought from authors. A key issue in the commissioning process is that the editor clearly communicates to the writer what is wanted. When an editor has a regular pool of writers a mutual understanding can be achieved. However, when the writer is new to the process, the editor will need to take some time explaining general issues such as style and tone, as well as the specific needs for the particular piece of writing.

The key policy consideration is to decide whether content will be commissioned internally, or whether there will be a budget to commission some content from freelance authors. The implications of an internal-only commissioning policy are that:

- staff may not have all the writing and editing skills to create enough quality content. Training can partly solve this problem, although it will not do so immediately, nor will it turn someone who has no feel for writing into a good writer;
- staff may simply not have the time to create the required content. This could be solved by hiring or by a realignment of job functions.

The implications of using freelance authors are that:

- the editor will require at least some experience in finding and selecting freelance writers;
- this can be a time-consuming process;
- they can plug content gaps efficiently and cost-effectively, but it becomes an expensive process where large quantities of content are required;
- they will rarely understand the organization as thoroughly as its own staff. In any freelance projects, it's important that the freelance writer work closely with staff who have a detailed understanding of the subject;
- they may move on to work elsewhere. Consistency is therefore lost and familiarizing a new writer with the subject will cost money;
- the editor will require a budget.

Calendar of events

A calendar of events allows for the more efficient management of the commissioning process. It tracks the content that needs to be created for important forthcoming events. Events can include the launch of a new product, a report from the quarterly sales meeting, the restructuring of HR policies, or expansion within a particular region. A calendar of events should look ahead at least a month and perhaps even a year.

It is the role of a particular editor – with input from the managing editor – to create and manage the calendar of events. The type of things to be tracked will include:

- event or subject name;
- brief description of what is required;
- number of words required;
- writer/author responsible;

- extra material required (images, audio, etc.);
- due date for copy;
- resource requirements;
- where the content will be published (intranet, extranet, internet);

A simplified version of the calendar of events can be posted on a wall in a basic calendar format, specifying simply the event/subject and date. Such information could also be placed on an intranet. An important effect of this approach is that it can encourage writers to get in touch with the editor with proposals, rather than the editor constantly having to figure out who should write what.

As any experienced editor will tell you, the commissioning process is rarely as simple as it seems. Writers are notorious for waiting until the last minute to get working on their copy. They may require regular pep-talks to make sure they are on track. Commissioning can therefore be time-consuming for the editor.

ACQUIRING CONTENT

Not all content can or should be created in-house. Creating all your own content can be a much more expensive process than acquiring at least some of it from third parties. Ways of acquiring content include linking to third-party sites, buying it and partnering with other organizations.

One of the most efficient and cost-effective ways of creating content on the Web is by linking to content on other websites. Linking is one of the foundations upon which the Web is built, and used properly it can deliver real value both to the reader and the organization. Yahoo is just one example of a successful business built on the linking model.

Checklist: linking to third-party websites

- Review – If you are linking to another website, make sure to review it carefully. Remember, linking is like embedded word-of-mouth. You are advising readers to spend their time going to another website with the expectation that it will have the content the reader requires.

- Don't over-link – the reader does not want to be presented with a long page of links. Be selective; show the reader only the very best links.

- Don't over-link to one particular website – the legal issues with regard to linking are not fully clear. However, it is often seen as an infringement of copyright if you create a whole series of links to another website.

- Be careful with "deep linking" – while it is acceptable practice to link to a section in a website, such as the homepage or a product section, you need to be careful with regard to linking to a specific document. It's difficult to advise on policies here, as the area is quite gray. However, as a general rule of thumb, if you are deriving significantly more value from linking to a website than that website is getting from you linking to them, there could be a problem.

- Avoid frames – this is a general rule. However, framing is particularly to be avoided with regard to linking to other websites. If the reader links to another website and carries with them a frame of your page, then it can be claimed that you are "passing off" another website's content as your own.

Purchasing content is also an option. There may well be news feeds, reports or other material that can provide valuable content for your website. It is often cheaper to pay copyright fees for these than to write the content from scratch.

However, you should be careful about the percentage of purchased content you use. Unless you are purchasing content under an exclusive contract, in which case it may prove to be prohibitively expensive (unless you have a huge readership), over-use of purchased content may give a generic and bland feel to your publication.

READER-CREATED CONTENT

A key difference between Internet publishing and traditional publishing is that the Internet invites much greater reader interaction. Reader-created content is made possible through software such as mailing lists, discussion boards, chat and customer review boards.

Reader-created content encourages reader participation and feedback, and is a cost-effective way to add content to the website. It also builds a sense of community that will generate repeat visits and a sense of loyalty.

Reader-created content tends to be most effective on community-oriented or entertainment-oriented websites, or on websites where you want to encourage the free flow of ideas and interaction. On more corporate-oriented websites, it tends to be less useful.

It's important to understand that if you create an environment where readers can contribute content, this can end up giving a lot of power to the reader. The reader might start putting in comment that is not always favorable to the organization. It is therefore very important to establish clear policies and procedures with regard to how these environments will be managed. In particular, a clear policy statement needs to be made available to all readers who wish to contribute content.

A special section in the terms of use statement needs to be made available to any reader who wishes to contribute content. If the reader is required to fill out personal information before they can use the chat software, for example, they should be advised to read the terms of use before they are allowed to use the software. It should cover:

- copyright with regard to the content contributed;
- all libel and legal issues;
- termination conditions.

The importance of the moderator

Moderators are like editors; they carry out a quality control function on the content submitted by readers. Furthermore, a moderator combines the skills of an editor and chairperson. Moderation of mailing lists, discussion boards and chat are essential for the following reasons:

- Without an enthusiastic moderator it is almost impossible to get a vibrant and useful mailing list, discussion board or chat environment up and running. A quality moderator will introduce new and interesting topics if there is a deficiency of such topics from the readers' point of view.
- A good moderator will give focus to reader-created content, sifting through the contributions and publishing only the most relevant

ones, and will ensure that the discussions and contributions are about the topic.

■ The moderator acts as a referee to readers who may have come into conflict, and will police content from a copyright and libel point of view.

Email mailing lists

An email mailing list is a system that allows you to create, manage and control the flow of content between a group of readers. With a mailing list readers can send messages that other readers who have subscribed to the mailing list can read.

Mailing lists allow for the discussion of more complex ideas which take time to work through, and can become a channel for positive ideas for the organization in relation to improving its products and services. They allow readers to send each other regular email on a particular pre-defined range of topics, and bring together a group of experts, who may live far apart, to discuss actively a topic over a long period of time.

The best way to explain the benefits of a mailing list is through an example. Let's say you want to get a discussion going on the direction of a product. You could establish a mailing list, select a moderator and invite contributions. People on the list would contribute their ideas by email. These would go to the moderator who would judge their quality. Depending on the publication schedule, the moderator would send out a digest of the best contributions. This digest would hopefully spark more ideas and more contributions. The mailing list gets a life of its own as product ideas and features are discussed and explored.

The mailing list gets a life of its own as product ideas and features are discussed and explored.

Checklist: recommendations for email mailing lists:

A mailing list is in essence another form of subscription-based publishing, which is examined in greater detail in Chapter 10. However, here are some high-level recommendations for managing mailing lists:

■ Moderate.

■ Plant the lists with interesting content that will provoke discussion.

- State clearly the mailing lists' main aims and give some example subjects.
- Give a call to participate.
- Give information on how to subscribe and unsubscribe from the list.

Discussion boards/newsgroups

Discussion boards (also known as bulletin boards, newsgroups, forums, discussion groups) are published on a website, and allow people to read all the messages left by other people on a particular topic and post new or follow-up messages. Discussion boards are more casual than email mailing lists. The reader can read what's being discussed without having to subscribe.

An effective adaptation of the discussion board approach is the way Amazon.com encourages reader reviews. Basically, if you have read a particular book you can go to Amazon and write a review of it. This is helpful to other readers who are thinking of buying that book.

Online chat

Typically these "real-time" discussion areas involve a relatively small number (between 2 and 20) of people at any one time. By their very nature they tend to be far more ad-hoc, spontaneous and informal than discussion boards or mailing lists.

This real-time form of communication means online chat tends to be more appropriate for socially-oriented websites such as entertainment sites. It is also suitable for one-off events such as online focus group meetings, brainstorming meetings within your own organization, and "meet the expert"events.

Checklist: recommendations for discussion boards and online chat:

- Moderate.
- Encourage contributions that are about the topic.
- Don't encourage anonymity, impersonation or personal attacks.

- Don't allow profanity or spam.
- Inform contributors about all legal issues.
- Give contributors clear contact details (phone and email) that they can use if they see any content that might violate the above points.

FIGURE 5.3

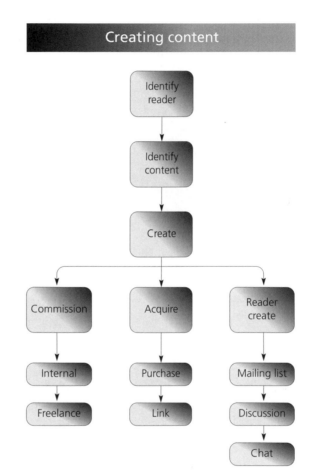

Content is what the Web is about. As this chapter has shown, its creation is a complex process, from the first steps of identifying your readers and your content types through the commissioning and acquisition processes to the development of reader-generated content. Time spent thinking through these issues and applying the checklists to the content on your site will pay big dividends for your site and for your readers.

In future chapters, as we move on to content editing and publication, it's useful to remember the old adage that says you can't turn a sow's ear into a silk purse. The best-staffed, best-designed and most technologically advanced website will be a failure if the content isn't any good to begin with. Equally, if you have targeted the wrong reader, it doesn't matter how good the content is – it's simply not what the reader wants, and your publication will fail.

Reference

Gerry McGovern, Rob Norton and Catherine O'Dowd, "The Web Content Style Guide," Financial Times Prentice Hall, September 2001

EDITING CONTENT

6

Many websites were launched without formalized systems of editing. Content was "put on the Web" by a webmaster, who typically had a technical background. The best websites learned of their need for editors the hard way – by finding that their content was poorly written, disorganized, and riddled with bad spelling and grammar.

Editing is about preparing content for publication. It is an essential quality control function. Editing is about making sure that the good stuff gets published and the poor stuff doesn't. It's about making sure that what is published reflects the publication scope, the key messages, the agreed style and tone, etc. Good editing makes for a good publication. Poor editing makes for a bad one.

Much Web content is poorly edited, and as a result the Web is seen by a great many people as an environment of inferior content. (A major Forrester Research survey in 2000 found that 75 percent of respondents believed content on the Web was "poor quality.") If your readers take the view that your website has poor-quality content, you will lose their trust and custom.

Content is like the "rotten apple" syndrome. If a reader comes across one article that is clearly wrong, of inferior quality to what they expect, or is out of date, they will begin to suspect all your content. Remember, the reader is particularly skeptical on the Internet. They know very well that the Web gives everyone the opportunity to publish, with the result that there is an incredible amount of junk out there.

Quality content is at least as critical within an intranet website as it is on a public one. Unfortunately, because the intranet is not in the public domain, content standards are often ignored. For example, if staff use an intranet to locate an HR policy document, they expect that document to be accurate and up to date. If it is not, the value of the intranet is severely diminished in their eyes.

Quantity is often the enemy of quality publishing. Less is invariably more.

A basic rule of publishing is that it's much better to publish 500 documents of high quality than 5,000 documents of which 500 are high quality. Quantity is often the enemy of quality publishing. Less is invariably more. This applies not just to the number of documents you publish, but the documents themselves. There has rarely been a 2,000-word document that cannot be made better by editing out 500, if not 1,000, words. Always keep in mind that quality editing is as much about what you don't publish as what you do.

CONTRIBUTING CONTENT

One way in which publishing on the Web differs from print publication is what we call the "contribution" process. Contributing is about getting content that has been created by staff, acquired from third parties or generated by readers, to an editor. In a Web environment, contribution is not simply about delivering the content to the appropriate editor. It is also about making sure that the appropriate metadata has been attached to the content.

Metadata sounds complicated but it's great stuff. Without it the potential value of content on the Web is severely limited. The Web has billions of documents. How are readers going to find the right one? Readers are tired of getting thousands of search responses, a great many of them irrelevant to the content they are looking for. Metadata is about making sure that the reader can quickly find the exact content. (Metadata is dealt with in detail in Chapter 7.)

In our information overloaded world, metadata is not just something that would be nice to have. It is *essential*. We should see metadata as an extension of the "grammar" of the document. A good author will spend time checking their grammar and spelling. In a Web environment, a good author will add their metadata, because if the metadata is poor or wrong, then the chances of the right reader finding the content are greatly reduced. If content does not reach its intended readership then it has failed. It has created zero value. In this day and age nobody wants to be creating zero value.

As a general rule it is a good policy that the author who creates the content is also the person who contributes it, as they will be much better qualified to fill out the relevant metadata. However, the author may be too busy to contribute. If the document is to be contributed by someone other than the author, this person should have an understanding of the content – if they don't understand it they won't be able to create the appropriate metadata for it.

How the contribution process works

Let's say an author wishes to create a technical document on the braking system of car X. They will probably create this document with a word processing software tool such as Microsoft Word. Having completed the document to a point where they feel it is ready for their editor to see, they are ready to contribute it. (If they do not wish to contribute it, then a contributor needs to be informed that the document is now ready for contribution.)

In a traditional publishing environment, contribution is relatively straightforward. The author physically sends a copy of the document to their editor. That can happen with a Web publication too. But it is an inefficient and expensive process. As Varian (1997) estimated, if an electronic editorial process can be established, the associated processing costs can be reduced by as much as 50 percent.

If an organization needs to publish large quantities of content on a regular basis, managing that content by a physical process is neither efficient nor cost-effective. Therefore, some form of "content management" software system is necessary that allows as many publishing processes as possible to be dealt with electronically.

For the person contributing a document of content, the process will involve them putting this document into a document template. This template asks for the relevant metadata, such as heading, summary, author, date of publication, classification, editor, etc. Once the contributor has filled out the metadata it is ready for contribution.

EDITING CONTENT

The actual editing process involves preparing a document for publication. It is essentially a quality-control function for content. It is a fundamental rule of publishing that nothing should be published without going through an appropriate editorial process.

The key issue in designing an editing process is to decide how extensive it should be. When you are dealing with large quantities of content, it is an extremely time-consuming, complex and expensive process to ensure that every document will be word-perfect every time. Implementing too rigid and convoluted a process will result in considerable expense. It may also mean that it will take a long time to get each document published.

However, if the editing process is too flimsy then poor-quality content will inevitably be published on the website. This is even worse, as the reader will simply not read the content and the whole publishing exercise will have come to nothing. A balance needs to be achieved between developing an overly-complex editing process and one which is so simple as to be useless.

The type of editorial process required will be heavily influenced by the type of content being created and the type of reader it is being created for. Let's take the example of the technical document on the braking system for car X. This document may not have to exhibit the best writing style in the world. However, it is absolutely essential that it is accurate. As a broad rule of thumb, you could say that the editing process for an intranet or extranet looks for content that is technical, factual and detailed, whereas the editing process for an Internet website looks for short, punchy and eye-catching content.

The three key editing functions

Editing responsibilities are poorly defined at many websites. In print publications, the roles of editors are well understood and have been formalized over decades – sometimes centuries. At a glossy magazine, for example, written content goes through four or more levels of editing before it's printed. At newspapers, even late-breaking news must go through two or more levels of editing.

Too many websites are still struggling to put out quality content without a formal editing structure.

Successful websites have created the kind of editing hierarchies that exist in the offline world, and today the best websites are as slickly produced as the best print publications. Too many websites, however, are still struggling to put out quality content without a formal editing structure.

The job titles used to describe editors vary among different types of publications, and even from publication to publication. At *Time*, the largest US magazine publisher, the senior editor at a magazine is referred to as the managing editor. At *The New York Times* newspaper, the senior editor is called the executive editor, while other publications prefer the title of editor-in-chief. In the US, editors responsible for "line editing" (making sure text reads smoothly and logically and is free from grammar and spelling errors) are called copyeditors. In Britain, they're called subeditors.

We will discuss responsibilities, skills and nomenclature of editors in Chapter 11, but whatever terminology is used to describe editors, however many a publication employs, and no matter how they are organized, there are at least three basic functions that editors must perform. First, they must be responsible for the overall content of a publication/website, and for its look and feel. Second, they must be responsible for assigning or acquiring content for the publication, and making sure of its quality. Finally, they must ensure that the content is understandable, readable and free from error.

For convenience, in discussing editing tasks for a website, we will define the three functions as those of the managing editor, editor and copyeditor.

Managing editor function

The managing editor function involves responsibility for all major decisions – including, but not limited to, what kinds of content go on the website; how long articles should be in general; how the website is structured; how often content is updated; and what the general rules will be for headlines, fonts and graphics.

The managing editor function is best performed by a single person with near-absolute power, at least at the operational level – disputes will always arise between editors and writers over which articles should be published, whether they're too long or short, and whether they need to be rewritten or thoroughly edited. Editors and designers will often disagree on the amount of onscreen space that should be devoted to text and graphics. Ultimately, one person must be the final arbiter. The time pressures of publishing typically preclude long debates and committee approaches.

For large and complicated organizations, a good way to provide oversight of the website in general and for the managing editor in particular is to create an "editorial board" that includes representatives from all the organization's key constituencies. A large corporation with an intranet, for instance, would at the very least want an oversight board that included representatives from the company's operating units – marketing, human resources, legal and finance.

Once policy is set by the editorial board, however, it's important that the person filling the managing editor's role has broad operational authority for implementation.

Editor function

The editor function involves broad authority for the nature and quality of content. Editors should be empowered to commission content from writers (or to acquire it from third parties), and should have wide latitude in deciding basic questions of length, tone and scope. The editor determines whether a piece of content must be rewritten, and must be able to rearrange and rewrite the content if needs be. The editor should also be responsible for arranging for any graphics to accompany the article.

When the editor has approved a document for publication, the contributor and the author should be notified of the publication date and ideally the URL under which the document is to be published. If the document is not of a sufficient quality it is rejected and is sent back to the author. If this happens a note explaining why it has been rejected should be attached.

Authors are delicate creatures at the best of times. A great many people become particularly sensitive when someone criticizes their writing. It is therefore important that the editor is professional when rejecting content. Don't say, "This is the worst thing I've read in weeks." Do say, "There are some good ideas here, but they need strengthening." It may be that in certain circumstances the editor will phone or go to see the author if nearby to explain why the document was rejected. Remember, the editor should also be a teacher, helping people improve their writing skills so they will create better content in future.

The editor needs to ascertain whether the content contains useful information that is right for their reader. Key questions that need to be answered are – is it right for the reader? Is it suitable for publishing? Is it in line with publishing strategy? Does the content follow editorial policies? Is it accurate? Is it legal? If the editor has worries about legal issues, it should be routed to the legal department for advice.

Next comes style and tone. Does the writing style conform to the overall tone of the publication? Are the sentences, paragraphs, and the article itself the right length? At this point the editor may send the content back to the writer for revision, may rewrite the content to improve it, or make minor improvements, tightening up the style and tone, reworking the summary, changing the heading to be more punchy and descriptive, and ensuring that the way terms are used reflect how these terms are described in the glossary.

Copyeditor function

The copyeditor function is the final step in ensuring that the content is understandable and readable. The person filling this role may rearrange sentences and paragraphs and rewrite them to eliminate awkwardness and imprecision. The copyeditor should also check spelling and grammar. The copyeditor ideally should act as the champion of the reader, looking at each piece of content afresh and eliminating impediments to readability. During copyediting the metadata should be checked to ensure that it is all accurately filled in. Questions that need to be answered include – is the document classified correctly? Has the other metadata been assigned correctly (author name, publication date, etc.)? Are the keywords appropriate?

At a news site producing a large volume of original content, the three editing functions – managing editor, editor and copyeditor – may be spread across a staff of dozens; at a small website, a single person may have to juggle each role at different times. But each must be performed religiously to ensure the content is as accurate as possible.

FIGURE 6.1

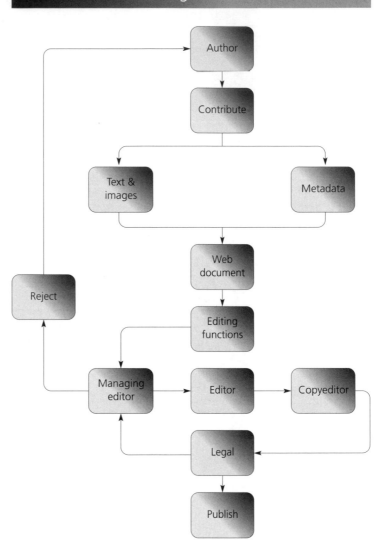

Editing content

Over time, some published content will become out of date and will therefore need to be removed from the website. (It is not simply content which requires review. On a periodic basis, defined by the managing editor, the content classification system, navigation and layout need to be reviewed, to ensure they are up to date and relevant.)

This is not a problem that traditional publishers had to face. Many newspaper editors were glad that after a few days their newspaper was used to wrap fish. Basically, the fact that a paper disappeared from public view after a week or so meant that what it said in January could not be easily compared with what it said in July.

This is not the case on the Internet. A published document stays published until the editor actively decides to remove it from publication. Much of the information overload on the Internet today is due to documentation that is out of date but has not been updated or removed.

There are a number of ways you can design a review process. First, you can have an expiration metadata field for the document in the document template. This is useful for event-type content where it can be precisely worked out when the content will become out of date. However, for a great deal of content it is not possible to decide in advance when it will be out of date.

Much of the information overload on the Internet today is due to documentation that is out of date but has not been updated or removed.

The second approach is to review already published content against new content that is about to be published. For example, if the document you wish to publish on the braking system for car X is an update on a document already published, then it may be that the already published document needs to be removed once the new document is put out.

In this sort of situation, it is appropriate for the editor to check the classification under which the new document is to be published to ascertain what documents are already published under this classification. Documents that become out of date as a result of the new document can then be

removed, or clearly flagged to indicate that they represent an earlier contribution on the subject.

A periodic review process of all content on the website needs to be
planned as well. Content should be reviewed on a yearly basis, or after a
major development or strategic shift. An example of what happens when
you don't have a review process was found on the White House website.
In March 2001, two months after George W. Bush had been sworn in as
president, the website was still making the following statement: "John
Quincy Adams: the only son of a president to serve as president himself."

It is critical to understand that incorrect content throws into question
the rest of the content on the website. Readers may forgive one mistake,
but if you keep presenting them with incorrect content they will lose faith
in the entire publication.

FIGURE 6.2

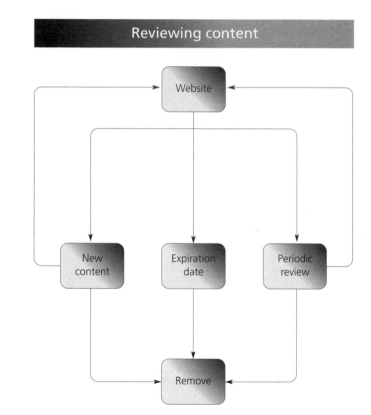

Regardless of how professional an editing process is in place, there will always be times where inaccurate or illegal content is published on the website. The organization requires an efficient process for correcting or removing such content.

The seriousness of errors that can occur in published content can range from minor to extreme. However, regardless of the type of error, once it is noticed the editor must be made immediately aware. The editor must then make it a priority to correct the error. This is particularly important in the case of libel and copyright infringement. The quicker the incorrect content is corrected/removed, the less of a case in law the injured party has.

The editor needs to make a judgment on the seriousness of the error. If it is minor then it may be sufficient to correct the document without any notice being placed in the document that a correction has been made. If the error is regarded as more serious then a note needs to be added to the top of the document explaining the error and the correction made.

If the error is deemed to be very serious, then the necessary corrections need to be made immediately. Also, a notice should be publicized in a prominent position on the homepage (ideally top of the right column), under a heading such as "Apology." It is up to the editor to decide how long such an apology should be left up on the homepage. This will depend on the seriousness of the error and the publication schedule. The more serious the error and the slower the publication schedule, the longer the correction should remain.

If the document was also distributed via an email newsletter, then the correction, depending on how serious it is, may also need to be distributed in the next issue of that newsletter. If the document was sold or distributed to another media, again, depending on the seriousness of the correction, those media may need to be informed.

FIGURE 6.3

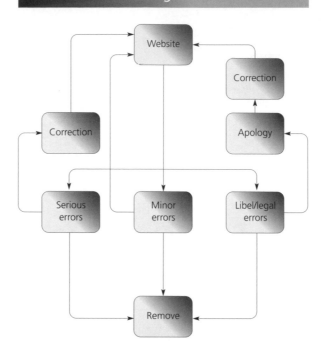

Correcting content

CONCLUSION

Even the best writer needs an editor. Good editing is what sets the best publications apart from the rest. Editing is also the publication's central quality-control function. Making sure that the three key editing functions – those of the managing editor, editor and copyeditor – are being performed consistently will give your website a professional feel, and your readers will thank you.

Periodically, all content on the website needs to be reviewed to ensure that it is still relevant. If not, it should be deleted. The publication needs to have a policy for dealing with errors and corrections – being slow to act can have significant legal consequences.

THE FOUR PILLARS
OF INFORMATION
ARCHITECTURE

7

Publishing is about getting content in front of your reader. In addition to the processes that online publishing shares with print publishing and which have already been covered – creating and editing content – online publishing involves a range of additional issues, specifically in relation to how content is organized and laid out.

The term "information architecture" has emerged to describe many of the issues relating to the organization and layout of content. Over the next three chapters we examine what we call the four pillars of information architecture: metadata and classification; search; navigation; layout and design.

In this chapter we examine the critical role of metadata and classification, and search. Chapter 8 examines how to create quality website navigation, while Chapter 9 looks at best practice in Web content layout and design. Together, these three chapters explore the central issues involved in publishing a website that is truly content-centric.

FIGURE 7.1

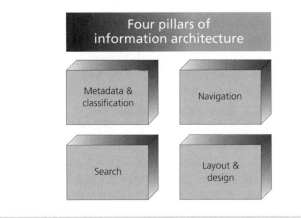

The heart of professional website design is the way its content is organized and laid out. This is a structural, architectural issue. In fact, a new discipline called information architecture is emerging to address the specific problems of website design.

Website design is not about graphical design. Many graphic artists dislike the Web because it is so limited a medium from a graphics point of view – screen resolution is poor, rich images are slow to download. Some graphic artists try to force the Web to be what it isn't, by designing visually-rich environments that result in a long, frustrating wait for the reader as the page downloads. The reader is faced by what they don't want – a big graphic – when what they came to the website for was to find content quickly.

In the hierarchy of a website publication the editor should come first, followed by the information architect, then by the graphic artists. Allowing it to happen any other way – which was often the case in the Web's early evolution – is asking for trouble.

The term "information architecture" describes how the content on a website is organized and laid out. The complexity of information architecture depends on the quantity of content being dealt with. Think of a building. If it is a one-room structure, the architectural planning is relatively simple. However, if it is a skyscraper with 80 stories and hundreds of rooms, the architectural complexity is much greater. So too with content. If the website has only 20 documents, then the architecture is relatively simple. However, if there are thousands of documents, the architecture becomes exceedingly complex.

So far, information architecture has evolved in a very haphazard manner. Websites have been initially built like one-room structures. As more content became available, more "rooms" were added as "extensions" to the building. As any architect or builder can tell you, there is only so far you can extend a given structure before things become unworkable. The result is that many websites had to be "trashed" after a short period and a new website built. In many situations, this "trash and build again"approach has happened not once but several times. This is clearly an unsatisfactory and expensive approach.

Information architecture does not simply deal with the architecture for a particular website. It also seeks to create a logical linking between a group of related websites, where appropriate. For larger organizations this is a key problem. These organizations often have dozens – sometimes hundreds – of websites, many with no cohesive relationship to each other. The result is a disorganized mess. It's like establishing a town and letting people build whatever they want wherever they want. Towns developed this way become disorganized, unworkable and ugly.

The primary function of an organization is to organize people and resources around a specific set of objectives to achieve a defined set of results. If organizations are not professionally organizing their content in an increasingly information-driven economy, then they are falling down on a fundamental function they are supposed to carry out.

In short, the purpose of information architecture is to organize content into a cohesive and logical structure that can be easily managed by the organization publishing it, and easily used by the reader who needs it.

METADATA AND CLASSIFICATION: A WEBSITE'S FOUNDATION

"According to the old Hollywood adage, it's cheaper to re-shoot a scene than to waste time and money searching for the original film in the studio's vaults," *Fast Company* magazine wrote in 1998. "Today the digitization of everything has made Hollywood's headache everyone's business problem."

Managers may think that planning for metadata and classification is a low-priority activity that doesn't really concern them. They are wrong. Metadata and classification are an essential pillar, a foundation stone upon which a large website is built. Without proper metadata structures, the more the website grows the more useless it will become. The more content that is published on the website the more disorganized it will be.

Without good planning for metadata and classification, searching for content becomes like the proverbial search for a needle in a haystack – except that, every day, the haystack is getting bigger! If organizations want to create websites that function, that readers will use rather than click away from, they must pay particular attention to how they develop and implement metadata and classification.

Metadata: the content about content

Metadata is the information about a document, such as the heading, summary, keywords, author, publication date, expiration date. (Classification is in fact a form of metadata but because of its central importance in information architecture, we are treating it separately.)

Without metadata a document merely floats among 550 billion other documents. The chances of it being found by the right reader are greatly diminished.

Metadata can be thought of as the "content about content." It is essentially the *who, what, when, where, why* and *how* about a particular document. Metadata is like a passport for a particular document. It describes all the essential details about a document. Without metadata a document merely floats among 550 billion other documents. The chances of it being found by the right reader at the right time are greatly diminished.

The purpose of metadata is to:

- allow every document to be stored in its appropriate place in the information architecture;

- collect sufficient information on a document so that it becomes easier for the reader to find the exact type of content they are looking for;

- ensure that essential legal and/or administrative information is gathered on a particular document (copyright information, etc.), which will allow the organization to manage that document professionally and efficiently;

FIGURE 7.2

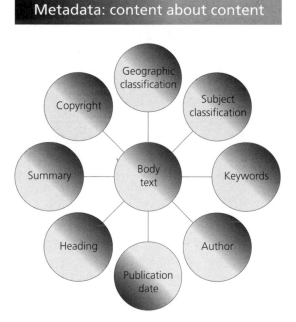

Metadata: content about content

- improve the chances of a particular document being indexed properly by external search engines, as some of these search engines will not index a website that does not have metadata.

General guidelines for metadata

The following guidelines should be followed when creating a metadata plan for a website:

- Talk to the reader before you design the metadata, as a primary function of metadata is to help the reader quickly find the information they want. Getting feedback on how readers like their content presented and how they would like to search is vital when designing appropriate metadata.

- Unless there is a specific reason against it, every page on the website should have appropriate metadata embedded in its HTML. Otherwise, that page will stand less of a chance of being found by both the internal search engine and external ones.

- Only collect the metadata that is truly useful. Metadata adds to the amount of work required in contributing a document. If you require an excessive amount of metadata on each document, the contributor may not fill out some fields or may fill them out hastily, thus generating errors.

- Metadata must be fundamentally linked into the advanced search process. Basically, the metadata collected will become the parameters for advanced search.

- Make sure that all essential information is collected. If "author" metadata is essential for copyright reasons, then make sure it is collected. Structure the metadata collection process so that the contributor cannot move the document to the next stage of publication if essential metadata has not been filled out.

- Inform contributors not to abuse metadata. If the "keywords" within a document are a metadata requirement then make sure that contributors enter only relevant keywords. Putting in popular or high-use keywords just to get your document returned in searches is counter-productive, as it frustrates the reader in the search for the content they are looking for.

- Make sure that there is a consistency of layout in the document templates used to collect metadata. For example, if the author name is the first field in template A, make sure it is the first field in all other templates, unless there is a logical reason not to.

Document templates

As we explored in Chapter 4, Extensible Markup Language (XML) is an approach or standard to collecting metadata that is becoming widely accepted. If the Internet is indeed a great big library with all the books on the floor and the lights turned out, XML is about turning the lights on and putting the books on the shelves in the right order.

Metadata, whether XML-based or not, needs to be collected through what are called "document templates." These allow for the structured and repeated collection of the metadata for a particular document type. Most organizations will have a small number of document template types. For example, in the financial sector there would be "morning note" templates, "industry report" templates, etc.

When creating document templates remember to keep the number small, or the contribution process will become confusing. Also, give the template a straightforward name such as "Morning Note," so the contributor will quickly recognize it.

Classification: expressing strategy in words

Classification is to business strategy what poetry is to prose. In the same way that poetry is (or should be) the absolute distillation of words, so too is classification the absolute distillation of strategy. Classification may historically have been regarded as something of relatively minor importance. In a Web-based world, however, it becomes something that must be championed at the highest level within the organization.

> **If the classification does not describe something of interest to them they will leave the website and be lost to the organization.**

When a reader comes to a website there are three things they are likely to do – read the content, search and examine the classification. If the classification does not describe something of interest to them they will leave the website and be lost to the organization. The top-level classification on your website is what will create a positive or negative first impression with your reader. It expresses, in the fewest possible words, what you do. (As we shall see from the following chapter, classification and navigation are very much intertwined.)

FIGURE 7.3

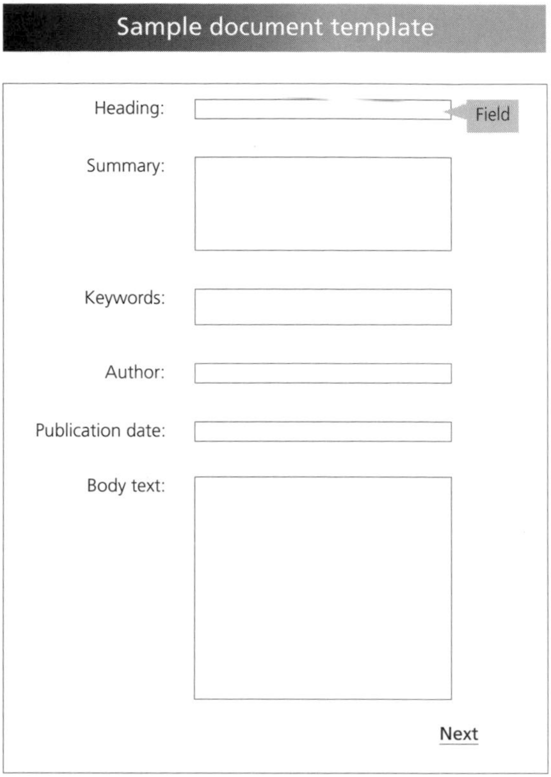

Sample document template

Heading: ☐ ◄ Field

Summary: ☐

Keywords: ☐

Author: ☐

Publication date: ☐

Body text: ☐

Next

Each of the fields needs to be filled in by the contributor. They can either enter the text directly, or "cut 'n paste" from a word processor or other package. The next stage in the contributor process will be to enter the classification for the document.

"Products," "Services," "Solutions." Which would you choose? "Products for large corporations," "Products for small and medium enterprises," "Products for home users." Which would you choose? "Germany," "United States," "Ireland." Which would you choose? These are classification decisions and they are central to what the organization does and how it describes what it does on the Web. Get your classification wrong and you will have a disorganized mess that will be of no use to anybody. In fact, poor classification, like poor content, will damage your reputation, making you look amateurish.

Thus the purpose of classification is to:

- articulate in precise text form the strategic focus of the organization;
- allow the organization to arrange content efficiently;
- facilitate the creation of quality navigation (see next chapter);
- help the reader get a proper context for the content (by context, we mean what else a particular piece of content relates to). For example, if you find a book by W.B. Yeats on Amazon.com, you will also find a classification-generated list of his other work.

Guidelines for better classification

It's relatively easy to classify 100 documents; 1,000 is much more difficult; 10,000 and over is very complex territory indeed. As we shall see from the following chapter, classification and navigation need to work hand-in-hand. It is no simple task to combine the logic of a classification system with the more marketing-driven needs of navigation.

While it is essential to have senior management involved in developing the top level classification, it is equally vital to seek professional expertise in developing the whole classification. These "information architects" are still scarce on the ground, and we will examine them in more detail in Chapter 11.

As with all publication design, the reader's perspective should be central to any classification design. This is particularly important when building on an existing classification. One fundamental question that must be asked is – does the reader understand the classification terms being used? If not, the whole exercise is futile.

The only way to classify for the reader is to involve them in the classification process. This will involve surveys and testing. Ask the reader what sort of top-level classification they would like to see. (The "top level" is the first level you see in a classification. Yahoo, for example, has "Arts & Humanities," "Business & Economy," etc.

Simplicity of design is the key to quality classification. Don't use jargon, ambiguous words or complex terms. If a simple word does the job, use a simple word. "Never use a long word where a short one will do," is one of the six classic rules of writing developed by British novelist George Orwell. It applies particularly to classification design.

In designing the classification levels, don't go more than five levels deep if possible. Aim for three levels as an ideal. The reason is two-fold. First, readers don't like repeatedly clicking down levels to get to the content they want. Second, contributors who have to classify the content can easily get confused and misclassify if there are too many levels.

Try to avoid having too many documents in a particular classification. More than 40 documents in any classification may indicate that it requires sub-dividing. It is important that the classification words and terms you choose for a particular level are all roughly the same length, as this makes it much easier to present them as navigation on the website. Use short words, where possible, as long classification terms can look ungainly when presented on a website.

Don't design your classification around the content you have now. Rather, create a design for the "whole" classification environment. Think about building design again. The owner of the building may have tenants for only 50 stories but believes that they can fill 100 stories over the coming years. Does the architect create a 50-story architecture or a 100-story one?

You may have content to fill out only a number of levels of the classification, but the long-term ambition of the publication scope may envisage much more content. Therefore it is vital for the information architect to have the long-term perspective in mind when designing the classification. With proper design the only classifications that will initially appear on the website will be those with documents in them.

A difficult question is how many classification terms to have at a particular classification level. The principle here is that, while neither is perfect, "clutter is preferable to clicking." If you look at successful websites such as Yahoo, Oracle, Cisco, AOL and CNN, you will see that they pack a lot into their homepages. This is to allow the reader to get quickly to the content they need. From a visual point of view, the aforementioned websites look cluttered. However, Web design must often compromise visual design to achieve optimal functionality. (Remember – the reader is always in a hurry.)

Ideally, there should be no more than 10 classifications at the top level, with a maximum of 15. (Yahoo has 14.) At lower levels, there can be a greater number of classifications, depending on the need. At heart classification design is a balance between creating an accurate classification, and creating something that a reader will not be overawed by when they see it.

FIGURE 7.4

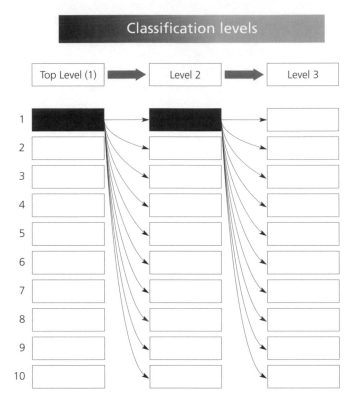

Getting the top level right is critical because it dictates how all the lower levels will be organized. We can see that each classification at the top level supports ten level 2 classifications. Equally, each Level 2 classification supports ten classifications at Level 3.

Seven steps in creating a classification system

Classification design requires detailed planning. It is also an iterative process. Rather than lock a group of people up in a room and wait for them to come up with the "perfect" classification, the key is to get out there and test, test, test. Here, we recommend a number of steps to take in classification design.

Step 1 – do your research. What sort of classification systems are currently in use throughout the organization? How are your competitors doing their classification? Are there any industry trends emerging? Talk to potential readers to get their views. Get a representative sample of content to see if there are any obvious classifications emerging.

Step 2 – design from the top down. Classification design should always begin at the top level. Get senior management and all key stakeholders involved. Set out to agree on a draft of the top-level classification. This can be done in a workshop environment with flip-pads and post-its. Picture the homepage and the classifications that would be presented on it. Brainstorm, but quickly move to eliminate duplication. Aim for an ideal of 10 top-level classifications, and no more than 15.

Step 3 – mock-up and test. Get together a very rough draft of the homepage. (In doing such mock-ups you are crossing over into navigation design, which we will explore in detail in the following chapter.) Don't worry too much about layout or design – just get the classifications and their order reasonably correct. Show it to senior management and stakeholders. If there is an editorial board, involve them. Show it to a selection of target readers.

Step 4 – iterate, iterate, iterate. Keep doing new mock-ups and testing until everyone is in agreement.

Step 5 – sign-off top level. It's essential that you get sign-off for the top level before doing too much work on lower levels. This is because if you change a classification at the top level it can have all sorts of implications for classifications at the lower levels.

Step 6 – work out the lower levels. This will involve more mock-ups and testing, and the need to draw strongly on the expertise of the information architect. Senior management should be involved in the final sign-off process.

Step 7 – review and get final sign-off. Make sure that everyone agrees with the classification and get final sign-off. Without final sign-off, further work on the website may become counterproductive.

Search functions on many individual websites are hopelessly inadequate. In our experience the majority are poorly designed and poorly maintained.

Search is a second pillar of information architecture. Search is one of the most critical and yet poorly designed features on many websites. While public search offerings such as Google and Yahoo are fighting to keep up with the vast quantity of content on the Web, search functions on many individual websites are hopelessly inadequate. In our experience the majority are poorly designed and poorly maintained.

Readers rely heavily on search but are frustrated by poor quality. Consider the following:

- A 2000 Roper Starch Worldwide survey found that 86 percent of respondents wanted a more efficient means of searching the Web.

- A 2001 survey by PricewaterhouseCoopers found that more than three-quarters of online shoppers in the US used a search function to find the products they needed. Some 43 percent believed that search functionality was the most important feature in online shopping.

- A 2001 study from NPD Group found that search listings were more effective than a standard banner or button advertisements when it came to brand recall, favorable opinion rating, and inspiring purchases.

- A 2000 study of American society, conducted by Lewis, Mobilio & Associates, found that respondents turned to the Internet and search engines first in their quest for information, and that they would be willing to pay $14.50 per week to find the right answers to questions.

How Web search works

When you search a website you do not actually search the "live" website itself, but rather an "index" of the website. The search software indexes the website to improve the speed at which search results are returned. There are two broad types of search options on the Web.

Basic search – sometimes known as "keyword search," this is a search facility for a basic query. This usually involves entering a keyword or combination of keywords.

Advanced search – here, the reader can do more complicated searches.

There are a few general standards that should be employed when developing search:

- Search should begin with the touch of the return key, as well as the click of the "Search" button.
- The ideal font for the search box is Arial, as Arial is a narrow font and allows the reader to enter more characters in a smaller space.
- Make sure the website is regularly indexed, so that search will be up to date.

Basic search

Search is something people do all the time on websites, so it should be immediately accessible. Basic search should be accessible from every page on the site. The emerging convention is to have the search box in the top right of the masthead, or near the top left, just underneath the organization's logo. (For information on mastheads, see Chapter 9.) Basic search should include:

- a search box, large enough to allow a minimum of 20 characters to be entered;
- a font size in the box of ideally 10 point;
- a button to the right of the search box labeled "Search";
- a text link close to the search box labeled "Advanced search" if available.

Advanced search

Advanced search is where metadata becomes truly useful. If, for example, content has author and date metadata, and has been classified by country and subject area, then the reader can refine their search very effectively.

For example, they could search for documents by John Brown, published between January and March 2001, under the subject area "PCs, relating to the German market, containing the keyword 'IBM.'" Such a search will greatly reduce the number of irrelevant results the reader will get, helping them home in on exactly what they are looking for.

FIGURE 7.5

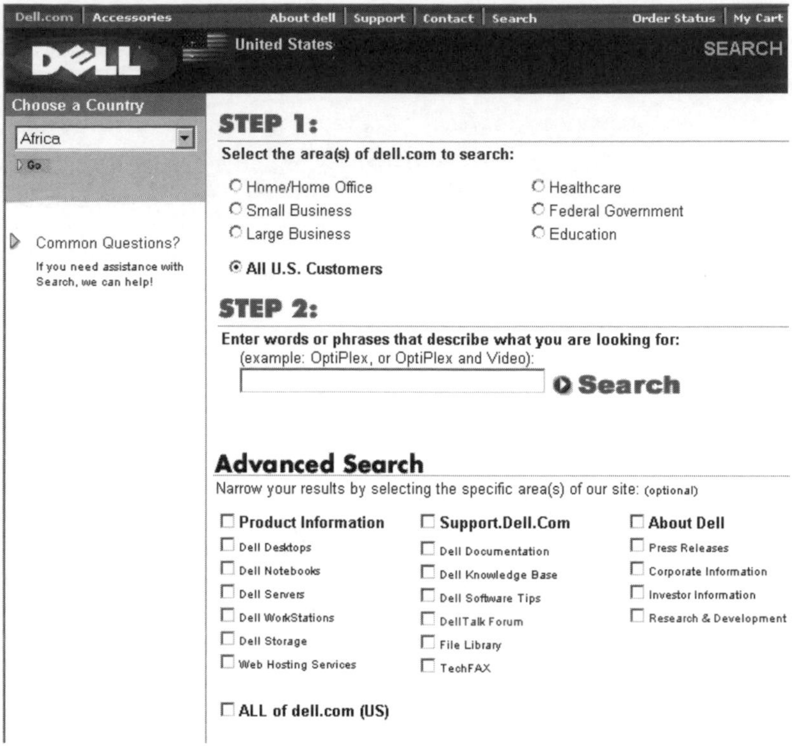

In its advanced search page, Dell gives the reader a wide range of options with which to narrow down their search.

Displaying search results

Simplicity is essential when displaying search results. The search results page will be one of the most looked-at on your website, so it needs to be well laid out. Remember, the reader is in the process of carrying out a very specific activity and they don't want to be distracted. Therefore the page should be almost bare, except for the set of results and the search box containing the keywords under which the reader made the search.

Each search result should ideally contain:

■ title/heading of the document/page, hyperlinked and in bold;

■ a two-line summary of the document/page;

- the URL for the document/page displayed unlinked on a separate line.
- the classification under which the document can be found, hyperlinked.
- the date of publication of the document.

FIGURE 7.6

Advanced Search   Preferences   Search Tips

metadata   Google Search

Searched the web for **metadata**.

Category: Reference > Libraries > ... > Technical Services > Cataloguing > Metadata

Metadata at W3C
... **Metadata** and Resource Description. **Metadata** is machine
understandable information for the web. The ...
Description: **Metadata** research at the World Wide Web Consortium.
Category: Reference > Libraries > ... > Technical Services > Cataloguing > Metadata
www.w3.org/Metadata/ - 3k - Cached - Similar pages

Dublin Core **Metadata** Initiative (DCMI)
... The Dublin Core **Metadata** Initiative is an open forum engaged in the development of
interoperable online **metadata** standards that support a broad range of ...
Description: Official page of the Dublin Core **Metadata** Initiative.
Category: Reference > Libraries > ... > Cataloguing > Metadata > Dublin Core
dublincore.org/ - 21k - Cached - Similar pages

Digital Libraries: **Metadata** Resources
... **Metadata** is data about data. The term refers to any data used to aid the identification,
description and location of networked electronic resources. Many ...
Description: IFLA collection of Internet **metadata** resources.
Category: Reference > Libraries > ... > Technical Services > Cataloguing > Metadata
www.ifla.org/II/metadata.htm - 101k - Cached - Similar pages

UKOLN **Metadata**
Metadata. UKOLN. Projects. We are participants in the following projects which
relate to resource description: ... Initiatives. ... Registries. ... What is **metadata**? ...
Description: Resources from the UK Office for Library and Information Networking
Category: Reference > Libraries > ... > Technical Services > Cataloguing > Metadata
www.ukoln.ac.uk/metadata/ - 6k - Cached - Similar pages

The Google search engine lays out its search results in a very reader-
friendly manner.

CONCLUSION

Just as architecture is thought through before the ground is broken for a new building, so should information architecture be thought through before you begin to build a website. Once the right questions have been asked – and answered – about metadata, classification and search, many of the other elements of website design will fall into place logically. Your readers will surely thank you by visiting your site more often, and you'll thank yourself for having established a foundation upon which you can build your site.

NAVIGATION CRITICAL

8

If content is the heart of every website publication, navigation is its brain, and a fundamental pillar of information architecture design. When dealing with large quantities of content, the critical importance of navigation cannot be overestimated. Content that can't be found can't be read. It's like the proverbial tree falling in the forest. If nobody hears it fall, does it really make a noise? If content can't be found and read, this means a lot of cost but zero value.

Navigation is the website's "table of contents." In a traditional publication you have page numbering to help you navigate. You can hold the publication in your hands and flick through it. If it's a large publication there is usually an index at the back that can be used.

You can't hold a website in your hands. You can't get an immediate sense of its size or complexity. You navigate a website one screen at a time. That can be very disorientating. It's easy to get confused, to get lost. A reader who gets lost or confused in this attention-deficit age is likely to hit the "Back" button. Therefore, creating a navigation system that makes the reader feel comfortable and allows them to find the content they want quickly is critical to the success of any website.

Think of how you use a telephone directory. You want to get a number as quickly as you can. Many of the most popular websites (Yahoo, Amazon, eBay) are like directories. Their strength lies in how quickly they can help the reader find what they came looking for.

Designing navigation is like designing a road-sign system. The over-riding design principle is functionality, not style. A reader on the Web, like a driver in a car, moves quickly. Numerous studies have shown that people "scan-read" on the Web, which means that their eyes dart quickly across text.

Navigation is never the end objective for the reader. It is there to help them get somewhere. (Most people don't stand around admiring road signs.) Navigation works best when the reader hardly knows it's there. Therefore, navigation design should always be simple, direct, unadorned, with the over-riding objective of helping the reader get to where they want to go.

Navigation and classification are very much intertwined. Where classification is the science of developing a logical order for how content is organized, navigation is the art of presenting the reader with the most natural and commercial paths through the content. Navigation is "commercial" in the sense that it will want to point the reader towards areas of the website where the organization can derive most value from the reader's visit.

There are two key conflicts that occur with classification and navigation:

- Classification seeks order and a system that will allow current and future content to be organized in a logical way. Sometimes the thinking about classification draws from archaic and complex order systems that are understood by librarians but are not very intuitive to the average reader. The primary objective of navigation design is to be as easy to understand as possible for the reader.

- Navigation is often driven by the need to sell, and/or by the ego of a particular department or product group. ("A link to *our* product *must* be on the homepage.") If navigation design ignores key principles of classification order, and is overly dictated by the needs of selling and ego, it will not seem natural for the reader, and nobody will win.

As always balance is key, and keeping the reader's needs as the driving force for both classification and navigation design is crucial. While the classification is designed first, it should not be designed in isolation to the needs of navigation. Unfortunately, both can take on political and emotional overtones. (People *do* get emotional about classification.)

It can be easy to give in, to accept an obscure classification approach because the librarian is arguing fervently for it, or to give that department head his link because he is friends with the chief executive – but that's a recipe for disaster. Compromise is always necessary. Just don't compromise on the objective of helping the reader quickly find the content they need.

Navigation and search are intertwined. Strictly speaking search is a form of navigation. In many situations, the reader will use a combination of the search function and some navigation options. Remember, most readers are "content gatherers." They will use search to bring them to the subject area or product type they are interested in. Then the navigation should kick in, giving them the context for their search.

Navigation design requires detailed planning. Once launched it is not something that should be chopped and changed at every whim. You should treat your navigation and classification as if they are "written in stone" because otherwise you risk confusing your regular readers (customers), and these are the people you should avoid confusing at all costs.

Think about it this way. You visit midtown Manhattan regularly. Your favorite clothing store is situated on Madison Avenue, which is a block from Grand Central Station. If the next time you head to Madison Avenue you find that a new street with a whole new set of shops has been placed between it and Grand Central, wouldn't you feel somewhat disoriented?

People are by nature habitual and conservative. If every couple of months you change the structure and navigation of your website, you will risk alienating regular visitors who have got used to your formula.

TEN PRINCIPLES OF NAVIGATION DESIGN

1. Design for the reader

The fundamental principle of navigation design is that you should design for the reader – the person who uses the website. Avoid designing navigation simply because it looks good. And avoid designing navigation from the point of view of the organization – using internal, obscure classification names that aren't commonly understood.

Remember, navigation is an aid for the reader, so unless you've engaged with them and found out how they like to navigate, it is difficult to design navigation that will meet their needs. What this means is that navigation should never be designed in a "lab" environment. Iterate! Iterate! Iterate!

When designing navigation:

- Involve readers from day one by surveying or interviewing them about how they would like to navigate the content.
- Create mock-ups of the navigation as early as possible and show them to a sample of readers to get feedback.

2. Provide a variety of navigation options

If everyone wanted to navigate through content in the same way, the job of the navigation designer would be a lot easier. Unfortunately, studies show that different readers have different preferences on how they like to navigate around a website. Therefore, to accomodate a variety of readers and their navigation requirements, a range of navigation options should be offered.

Some readers may want to navigate geographically. Some may want to navigate by subject matter. Some may have found themselves on a particular page as a result of a search process, and may want to get to the homepage. Some may want to read the most recent documents like the one they have just read.

No single navigation option will fulfill all the above wishes. Therefore, good navigation design provides the reader with a variety of navigation options wherever they are on the website. As we will see later in this chapter, there are at least a dozen common navigation options.

To deliver a variety of them to the reader, an approach involving multiple classification of content is required. The Dell website uses multiple classification well. A notebook computer is classified under "Notebooks & Desktops" on the homepage. However, if the reader has clicked on "Home & Office," they will be presented with a link to "Notebooks" on the Home & Office homepage. Notebooks are also classified by country (US, Germany, Ireland, etc.). This multiple classification allows Dell to provide a wide variety of navigation options to the reader.

To allow the reader to navigate the content in the way they wish:

- provide a variety of navigation options;
- use multiple classification.

FIGURE 8.1

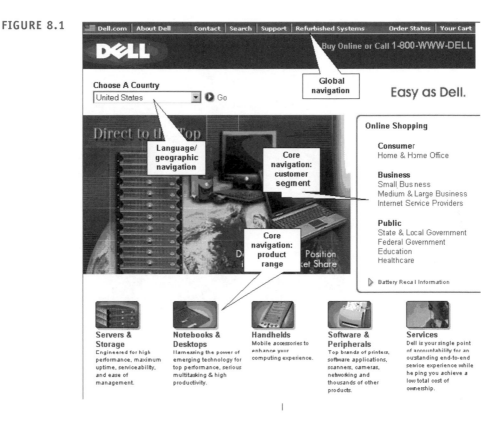

3. Let readers know where they are

Navigation should give readers a clear and unambiguous indication of what page of the website they are on. Web navigation is like a mixture of a map and a system of street signs. Imagine you are on holiday and you are looking at a map in a town square. If the map is well designed then one of the most prominent features will tell you – "You are here."

CNN supports the reader very well in this. For example, if you find your-self on CNN's entertainment page you will see in bold capitals in the masthead the word "ENTERTAINMENT."

FIGURE 8.2

Navigation should be presented as hypertext. However, where it is in graphical form – which is recommended only for global navigation – the classification name that describes the page the reader is on should be a different design from the other classifications in the navigation.

For example, let's say you are on the homepage of the IBM website. The "Home" classification in the global navigation is a different color from the other classifications in that navigation, thus indicating to the reader that they are on that particular page. (It should also be unlinked, because otherwise the link will loop to the same page.)

FIGURE 8.3

To let readers know where they are:

■ have prominent titles for every page to tell readers immediately what section of the website they are on;

■ make sure, if part of the navigation is in graphical form, that the link describing the page the reader is on is a different design to the other links in that navigation.

4. Let readers know where they've been

A fundamental principle of web navigation design is to let readers know where they've been on the website. This is a key reason to have as much of the navigation as possible in hypertext, rather than graphical, form.

With hypertext, when a link is clicked it changes color. The reason it changes color is so readers can know by looking at the navigation color scheme what sections of the website they have visited and what sections they have not. This will happen automatically if the navigation is presented as hypertext.

The standard colors for hypertext are blue for unclicked and purple for clicked. Avoid other colors. Navigation should always represent the familiar. On the vast majority of websites, blue and purple are the hypertext colors. The reader is used to these colors. Changing them for some visual design reason will serve only to confuse and disorientate the reader.

To let the reader know where they've been:

- keep as much navigation as possible in hypertext;
- use blue for unclicked and purple for clicked.

5. Let readers know where they are going

Navigation should let readers know where they are going. The obvious way to achieve this is to create classifications that are as self-descriptive as possible. Avoid building navigation based on classifications that are familiar only to those who work for the organization, unless, of course, your target readership is the organization's staff.

No matter how well the basic navigation is designed, there will be times when it requires extra support to provide greater clarity for the reader. There are a number of ways to achieve greater clarity:

- When readers click on a link they expect to go to an HTML page. If you intend them to go to a non-HTML page (PDF, Microsoft Word, audio, etc.), or to a password-protected area, inform them in advance. Tell them they will require a password. Tell them they are linking to an audio file, etc. Tell them the size of that file. Offer a link to a copy of the software required to listen to that file, just in case they don't have it.

- If readers click on a link they expect they will stay within the browser window they are currently operating within, unless you specifically tell them otherwise. Open new browser windows for a reader only when there is a compeling reason. There usually isn't.

- If the navigation element is an image, such as a company logo, and is linked to the homepage, put in ALT text that says something like "Company homepage." (ALT text is an HTML function that allows you to associate text with an image. This text will display when the cursor is placed over the image.)

FIGURE 8.4

As can be seen from the above example, if you hold the mouse over the Yahoo logo a rectangular box appears with the ALT text "Yahoo" in it.

- Change the color of the link when the mouse rolls over it. (A number of websites change the color and remove the underline as well, to add extra highlight. Red is a good color to change to. The CNN website does this well.) This is helpful when there are a lot of links close together. Because the link changes color, the reader knows exactly the link they are about to select.

At the Microsoft website, if you position the mouse over the "About Microsoft" link, it will change color from white to red.

- Consider drop-down navigation showing lower levels of the classification when the mouse rolls over a particular link. This allows the reader to jump deeper into the website if they wish.

On the Iomega website, if you position the cursor over the "products" link, for example, a drop-down menu will appear, allowing you to go straight to a selection of Iomega products.

FIGURE 8.5

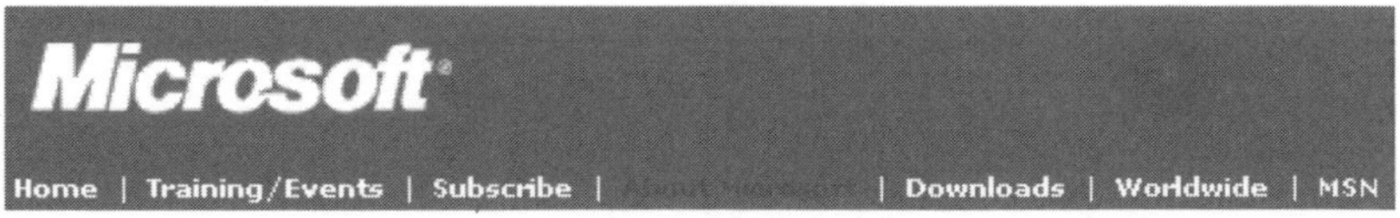

Microsoft®

Home | Training/Events | Subscribe | | Downloads | Worldwide | MSN

FIGURE 8.6

- Where the reader is asked to participate in a process, such as purchasing a product online, progress chart navigation can be helpful. This shows the reader how many stages there are in the process, and what stage they are at.

FIGURE 8.7   **1** SHOPPING CART   **2** ACCOUNT   **3** SHIPPING   **4** PAYMENT   **5** VERIFY   **6** CONFIRM

On the Iomega website there is a six-step purchase process. As you move through it a navigation chart shows your progress by extending a solid line, and changing the color of the completed steps.

- If the hypertext link is not quite as descriptive as it should be, put in Link Title text to give the reader more background. Link titles should be used only in exceptional circumstances, as navigation design should always strive to be as descriptive as possible. (Link Title is an HTML function that allows you to associate text with a link. This text will display when the cursor is placed over the image.)

6. Provide context

In a world of 550 billion documents, context is essential. Studies show that in the majority of cases, readers do not know exactly what content they need. If they do, they will invariably turn to a search process that offers them the quickest way to get to a particular document.

Navigation, on the other hand, gives readers context. It presents them with documents that are interconnected. It guides them and informs them of content the organization has that the reader might not have been aware of. This is what context is all about and it's what great navigation does in a seamless, easy-to-follow way.

A primary function of a homepage is to provide context for the reader. Homepage navigation is not simply about functional navigation such as hypertext and search. It also takes content highlights from the content archive, presenting them as summaries and/or features. Homepages are not just for the main page of the website. Every significant section, department or product group should have a homepage. (See feature and homepage navigation in the next section.)

Let's say that you go to the IBM or Dell website with a view to buying a notebook computer, but you're not sure what type. The navigation will quickly guide you to the homepage for notebooks, where the full range will be presented in summary form. If, for example, you choose to find out more on the Dell "Inspiron," then the navigation will guide you to the specific Inspiron homepage.

Links on the Inspiron homepage include "Rewards and Reviews." You may not have thought about looking for this type of content when you started your search, but once you see the link, you may well wish to see what sort of reviews this computer has received.

Related navigation also provides context. If, for example, you read an article on the CNN website, at the bottom you will find related articles and websites. This allows you to dig deeper if you wish. This is what good classification and navigation is all about – providing content in context that moves the reader in a positive direction. Traditionally, the sales rep would have casually informed the potential buyer as they examined the computer that such-and-such a magazine had recently given it an award. This vital work must now be done by navigation.

For navigation to provide the best possible context:

■ ensure that all content is properly classified;

■ alllow for a variety of product/section homepages that publish the most relevant and positive content for that particular product or section;

■ use related navigation that at the end of a document gives links to similar documents or websites.

7. Be consistent

If you are driving you get used not just to what the road signs say, but also their size, shape and color. If you are driving along following a set of signs and suddenly they change shape, size and color, your immediate response is one of confusion and hesitation. Thankfully, few countries change the design of their signs from region to region or town to town. Not so on the Web, where navigation can change in an ad-hoc manner within a particular website.

Readers particularly turn to navigation when they're confused or lost. Don't confuse them even more by displaying inconsistent or unfamiliar navigation design. For example, if you decide to put the core navigation in the left column, don't then switch it to the right column in another section of the website.

Consistency of classification is critical for successful navigation. This involves agreeing on a classification that eliminates all duplication and is rigidly adhered to. For example, don't classify a link "Home" in one section of your website and "Homepage" in another section. That serves only to confuse the reader. Establish the classification names at the beginning and use them consistently exactly as you have set them out.

Consistency of visual navigation design is equally important. Let's say your global navigation is in graphic form, and that you've used red buttons with white text on the homepage. This design should remain the same throughout the entire website. If you choose blue and purple for your hypertext navigation, don't change these colors in different sections of your website.

Navigation design requires:

■ consistent classification;

- consistent graphical navigation design;
- consistent hypertext colors.

8. Follow Web convention

Many people instinctively see the Web as a single medium. They like to carry over navigation skills that they acquire on one website to other websites – it makes life easier for them. In this sense, the more similar the navigation of your website is to that of other websites, the easier it is for the reader to get around your website.

Over time a number of navigation conventions have emerged on the Web. The designer who deliberately avoids these conventions to be different achieves nothing except confusion for the reader. Confusing the reader is the last thing quality navigation design should do.

There is an old saying in art that "geniuses steal, beggars borrow." This philosophy has a tremendous relevance for navigation design. Go to the biggest and best websites. See how they design their navigation and unashamedly imitate the best practice you find. Remember, conventional navigation design makes the reader more comfortable, thus more likely to purchase, or do something else positive.

Follow the navigation and classification conventions that have emerged on the Web. They include:

- Global navigation. This is navigation that runs across the top and bottom of every page, containing links to the major sections of that website. The convention is to begin the global navigation with a "Home" classification. Other commonly-used classifications include "About" and "Contact." (See Global Navigation later in this chapter.)
- The classification name "Home" is the convention for the name of the overall homepage.
- The classification name "About" contains content describing the history, financial performance, business focus, mission statement, etc. of the organization. Sometimes it's used in conjunction with the name of the organization. For example, "About Microsoft."
- The classification name "Contact" or "Contact Us" contains contact details such as email, telephone, geographic address and map location details.

- The classification name "Feedback" is used to encourage feedback from the reader.

- The organization's logo should appear on every page. It should be placed in the top left of the page and should be linked back to the homepage. It should not, however, be a link on the homepage itself.

- The name for the search facility on a website is "Search." The button or link that will initiate the search should also be labeled "Search." Search should also be initiated if the reader presses the return key. The term for more advanced search options is "Advanced search."

- The search box should be available on every page of the website. It should be placed on the far right of the masthead (see Chapter 9), or near the top left, just underneath the organization's logo.

- Every page should have a footer, containing global navigation as hypertext, contact, terms of use, copyright and privacy links. (See Chapter 9.)

- The colors for hypertext are blue for unclicked, purple for clicked.

- If the reader clicks on a link they expect to be brought to an HTML page. If it's anything else, such as an audio file, inform them in advance.

9. Don't surprise or mislead the reader

Never bring readers down a particular navigation path only to lead them to something they do not expect. Let's say that you're on holiday. You see a big sign saying – "Tourists: this way for free guidebooks." You keep following the signs until you reach the tourist office, only to find that these guidebooks are in German only. Unfortunately, there are websites where you navigate down through a set of links in one language, only to arrive at a document that is in an entirely different language.

It is not uncommon to go through a purchase process to find that the company ships only to a particular country. If this is policy, inform the reader as soon as possible clearly and prominently.

Never ask the reader to do something it is impossible or very difficult for them to do. A classic example is forcing all readers to fill out a "ZIP code" regardless of whether ZIP codes exist in that reader's country. Never offer the reader contact options they can't use. If you wish to deal with customers outside the US, for example, don't offer only "1-800" numbers that they can't call. Rather, make a statement such as – "For customers outside the US, please call …"

To avoid surprises for your readers:

- don't lead them down false navigation paths;
- clearly inform them of exceptions;
- don't ask them to do things they can't do.

10. Provide the reader with support and feedback

Strictly speaking, support and feedback are not navigation. However, they compliment navigation in an important way. The Web may well be the world's greatest library (with all the books on the floor and the lights turned out). However, there are two key navigation components of a library – a classification system and human support back-up.

If you don't know where the history section is or can't find that book on marketing, you can always ask someone. On any website, the reader should be only a click away from being able to contact the organization. Contact facilities may involve email, telephone, callback or chat support.

A "Help" link is particularly necessary where the reader is faced with a complex task. Help should be subject-sensitive, taking the reader to the topic relating to the page they were on when they clicked on Help. Examples of such complex tasks would be advanced search or a purchase process.

One way to support the reader without human intervention is to structure things in a way that helps them avoid making obvious errors. For example, if readers are being given a choice of actions, rather than having them type a response, let them choose by clicking on, or selecting from, a set of options. If you are asking them what country they're from, give them a country drop-down menu to select from, rather than asking them to write out the country name. If you are asking them their gender, give them a Male or Female selection option.

As humans we are used to receiving constant feedback as a result of our actions. If we touch something hot it hurts. If we pick up an item in a shop we may get a "feel" for it. If we make a mistake in our work someone will put us right. On the Web, however, the only viable immediate feedback is through text. Text must be used in a comprehensive way to inform the reader of the result of their action.

One way to support the reader without human intervention is to structure things in a way that helps them avoid making obvious errors.

For example, if the reader has filled out a 30-field form and clicked on "Submit," the website should provide the following type of feedback – "Thank you. Your form has been completed successfully." If, however, the form was not completed successfully, the feedback should isolate the particular error. It should not say, "Some fields in your form were not filled out correctly." Rather, it should say, "It seems that your email address has not been entered correctly."

Remember, many readers are unfamiliar with the Web, and even those with experience can become reticent, particularly when asked to input credit card details or when required to go through a process that is laborious. Always strive to make the process as simple and foolproof as possible. Explain every single step in precise, straightforward and friendly language. Use progress-chart navigation to show the reader how much of the process they have completed and how much there is still to do.

While it is essential to give as much feedback to the reader as possible, it is equally as important to encourage them to give feedback to the organization. Readers should be constantly encouraged to tell the organization what they thought of their experience on the website. Other options here include allowing readers to rate a particular piece of content they have just read by displaying for them a simple rating chart (1–10, excellent, good, fair, poor), and allowing them easily to inform someone else of important content by providing an "email this story" facility.

Reader support and feedback should:

- provide a contact link on every page;
- provide subject-sensitive help for complex tasks;
- ensure that the reader avoids making obvious errors;
- isolate errors the reader has made;
- provide progress chart navigation where processes are involved;
- provide options that allow the reader to give feedback.

When you're dealing with a lot of content, navigation design becomes very complex. The trick is to make it as simple as possible for the reader to use. Never underestimate the ability of the average intelligent person to make what often looks to a designer like the most obvious of mistakes. In life, it is often what is most obviously right that we avoid doing, and what is most obviously wrong that we can't help but do.

In navigation design the motto is – "So simple, even an adult can understand it."

Here is a navigation design checklist you can use to see how a particular website performs with regard to the 10 navigation design principles outlined.

Navigation design checklist

		Yes	No
Reader designed	Reader survey		
	Reader usability tests		
Navigation options	Classification path		
	Core		
	Document		
	Drop-down		
	E-commerce		
	Feature		
	Global		
	Homepage		
	Language and geographic		
	Personalization		
	Progress chart		
	Related		
	URL		
	Multiple content classification		
You are here	Prominent page titles		
	Changed navigation colors		

		Yes	No
You've been there	Blue/purple hyperlinks		
You're going here	Non-HTML page identification		
	New browser window identification		
	ALT text		
	Link color change		
Context	Proper classification		
	Product/section homepages		
Consistency	Consistent classification		
	Consistent graphical design		
	Consistent hypertext colors		
Familiarity	Global navigation on every page		
	Home, About and Contact links in global navigation		
	Home link first		
	Basic search on every page		
	Linked logo on every page		
	Footer on every page		
No surprises	No false navigation paths		
	Exceptions prominently highlighted		
	No impossible options		
Support and feedback	Contact links on every page		
	Help for complex tasks		
	Avoidance of obvious errors		
	Isolation of errors		
	Feedback options		

As we have already discussed, on a well-designed website you can find a document or page in a number of ways. That is what the reader wants. Readers think differently about how to find content, depending on their particular need at a particular time, and depending on their training, profession or habits. It's up to the organization to provide a set of navigation options that allow different readers to navigate to the document the way they want.

A website can offer readers at least 13 different navigation options. Not all of them are applicable to every website. However, a quality website should always offer a range of navigation options.

1. Classification path navigation

Classification path navigation is generally found near the top of the Web page, often underneath the masthead. This navigation shows the various parts of the particular classification tree in which a particular document or section of the website is located.

Let's say you arrive at the homepage of a website. The classification path navigation would display something like "**Home**." Clicking on the "Products" link would bring you to the Products page. The classification path navigation would then display something like "Home > **Products**." If you chose "Product XY" the display would show "Home > Products > **Product XY**."

FIGURE 8.8

Home > Arts > Humanities > History > By Time Period >
Ancient History

An example of a classification path navigation from the Yahoo website.

2. Core navigation

Core navigation is necessary where there is a large quantity of content on the website. An example of core navigation is "Arts and Humanities," at Yahoo. As a general rule the core navigation should be presented in alphabetical order. However, in certain circumstances, particular classifications may deserve more prominence, and can be brought to the top of the core navigation.

As much of the core navigation as possible should be presented on the first screen the reader sees when they load up the homepage. In general, the core navigation should be presented in the left-hand column. In directory-type websites or websites that have large quantities of content, it may be presented in the center column. It is rare to see the core navigation presented in the right-hand column.

FIGURE 8.9

Arts & Humanities
Literature, Photography...

News & Media
Full Coverage, Newspapers, TV...

Business & Economy
B2B, Finance, Shopping, Jobs...

Recreation & Sports
Sports, Travel, Autos, Outdoors...

Computers & Internet
Internet, WWW, Software, Games...

Reference
Libraries, Dictionaries, Quotations...

Education
College and University, K-12...

Regional
Countries, Regions, US States...

Entertainment
Cool Links, Movies, Humor, Music...

Science
Animals, Astronomy, Engineering...

Government
Elections, Military, Law, Taxes...

Social Science
Archaeology, Economics, Languages...

Health
Medicine, Diseases, Drugs, Fitness...

Society & Culture
People, Environment, Religion...

Yahoo core navigation.

3. Document navigation

This is navigation that occurs within a particular document, and is generally controlled by the author of the document. It will point to other key documents and/or websites. Document navigation should reflect appropriate use of hypertext. Those websites that simply convert documents from other media for publication on the Web rarely exhibit such navigation.

However, document navigation should not be overused. It needs to be understood that a link within a document is an invitation to leave that document. A way to get around this problem is by putting the links at the bottom of the document, or in the column to the right of the document.

4. Drop-down navigation

This is delivered by a drop-down menu. It is generally used as a space-saving device and to avoid too much clutter on a page. It is also used where you want to present an entire section of a lower-level classification tree. It needs to be understood that drop-down navigation acts as a support to the main navigation on the website. It should not be used as the main way of presenting navigation since it will show only one classification to the reader until the reader actually selects it. Global or core navigation should not be presented in a drop-down fashion.

5. E-commerce/shopping-cart navigation

A number of surveys have shown that many people fail to complete online purchases. A key reason is that they find the process too complicated or too long.

E-commerce or shopping-cart navigation allows the reader to move through a purchase process. It should be presented in a prominent position on every page, generally near the top or in the masthead. E-commerce navigation will include links such as "Shopping cart," "Checkout," "Your Account," and "Help."

A number of surveys have shown that many people fail to complete online purchases. A key reason is that they find the process too complicated or too long. The need to simplify e-commerce purchase navigation cannot be over-emphasized.

When designing e-commerce navigation:

- ask only for the information necessary to complete the purchase;
- test, test, test.

FIGURE 8.10

Amazon.com e-commerce navigation can be found at the top right of its masthead.

6. Feature navigation

This is temporary navigation that is used to feature some attractive content section on the website. For example, you might want to feature a new product that has been released, or a major promotion.

An example of feature navigation occurred during the 2000 Olympics and 2000 US presidential election. News websites had feature sections which allowed the reader fast access to content on these events. When the events were over, these features were removed.

FIGURE 8.11

Sydney 2000:

- Ian Thorpe leads 4x200 Australian relay team to gold world record
- Romania wins women's gymnastics title
- U.S. makes Olympic history in men's soccer
- Injury forces U.S. sprinter Inger Miller out of 100 meters

When the 2000 Olympics were on, CNN had a special feature navigation section on its homepage.

7. Global navigation

Global navigation should appear on every page of the website. It should contain links to the most important sections on the site. For small websites, global navigation may well contain links to all the top-level sections. It should be placed near the top of every page, usually in the masthead, and at the bottom of every page, as text links in the footer. In smaller websites, where there is no core navigation, global navigation is often found near the top of the page, in the left-hand column.

The first link in global navigation should be "Home." Global navigation should also contain the following links – "About" and "Contact." Global navigation should ideally have no more than eight links.

FIGURE 8.12

8. Homepage navigation

The primary function of the homepage is to give the reader context. It is vital that when a reader loads up the homepage they know exactly where they are. Therefore, key navigation such as search, global and core navigation needs to be immediately visible.

The homepage must act as more than a simple directory. It should highlight important content for the reader by way of feature navigation and by providing short summaries of important content. In this sense, the homepage is also "selling" to the reader the best and most exciting content the organization has to offer at any particular time.

9. Language and geographic navigation

The decision about which language a website should use is critical, and is directly influenced by the type of target reader. The choice of language or languages is not simply a strategic decision but may also have political elements. An important issue is whether to use American or British English. The dominant English on the Web is American, and those websites using British English who wish to target an American audience must consider this issue carefully.

If a substantial majority of readers use one language, then the homepage can default to it, with a choice of secondary languages available from global navigation. If the readers are more evenly spread between languages, then a preliminary or "intro" page must be created where the reader is asked to choose their preferred language.

Where a website is broken down by country or region, geographic navigation allows the reader to choose a particular country or region. A link to this navigation should be found in global navigation. In most circumstances geographic and language navigation can merge. For example, if you choose Germany, you are also sent to the German language version.

FIGURE 8.13

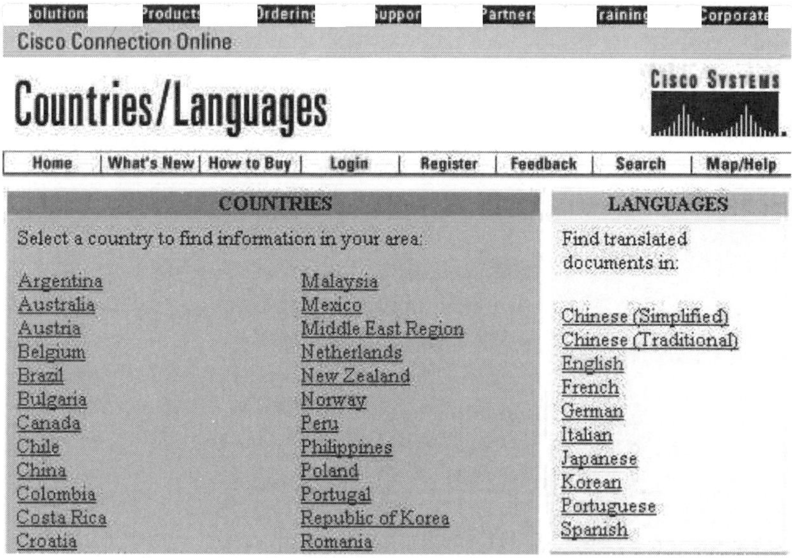

An example of language/geographic navigation on the Cisco website.

10. Personalized navigation

Personalization occurs when a reader decides how the website will look, in line with their own preferences, or when the organization changes the layout of the website to reflect a reader's previous usage.

Done right, personalization can be an extremely powerful tool. One of the best examples of personalization is the way that Amazon.com gives a reader book and music recommendations based on merchandise they have previously bought. However, personalization is costly and complex. A website requires a substantial quantity of content and a large number of readers before personalization becomes practical.

A survey published by Cyber Dialogue in May 2001 found that customers who buy more often and spend more online are attracted by personalization options. Not surprisingly, 87 percent of respondents got annoyed when a website asked for the same information more than once, while 82 percent were happy to give personal information once the website remembered it and properly addressed the privacy issue.

If taking a personalization approach, the reader should, where possible, have control over the process. It can be frustrating for them to have a piece of software make wrong assumptions about them. Personalize only what is necessary and useful. Tell the reader what information you are gathering on them.

FIGURE 8.14

Yahoo offers a very popular personalized service.

11. Progress chart navigation

Readers are impatient. If they cannot get an immediate sense of the length of the process they are likely to hit the Back button.

Progress chart navigation clearly shows to the reader in linear chart form the number of steps involved in a process, and the steps that the reader has already completed. It should be displayed prominently near the top of the page. Progress chart navigation is highly recommended at times when the reader is expected to complete any process that involves more than two steps.

Remember, readers are impatient. If they cannot get an immediate sense of the length of the process they are likely to hit the Back button. It is also true that many readers are hesitant and unsure when using the Web. Presenting them with a clear progress chart can make them more comfortable. Processes that progress chart navigation is useful for include purchasing a product and filling out a long form.

FIGURE 8.15

1 SHOPPING CART **2** ACCOUNT **3** SHIPPING **4** PAYMENT **5** VERIFY **6** CONFIRM

Progress chart navigation from the Iomega website.

12. Related navigation

Related navigation is found at the bottom of a particular document. It presents links to other documents from the same subject area. It helps the reader who wants more information on the subject to find related documents quickly. Related navigation can also provide links to other websites or other sections of a website that relate to the subject area.

FIGURE 8.16

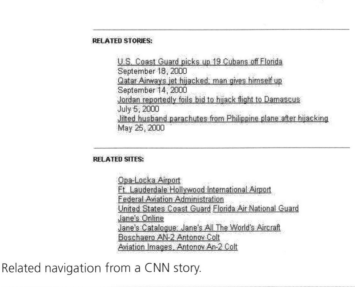

Related navigation from a CNN story.

13. URL navigation

URL (Uniform Resource Locator) navigation is found in the address box of the browser. To make it easy for people to navigate to your site using your URL, choose the shortest, most memorable URL possible for the website. If you are aware that readers commonly misspell your URL, register the misspelling, and then redirect that URL to the main URL. Choose lowercase for your URL, as this is what readers are accustomed to seeing. If the website has extensive content in a number of languages, then where possible get a URL for that country (.de for Germany, .ie for Ireland, etc.).

If the website has an extensive range of products, it may make sense to have a number of subsidiary URLs. For example, if you look for the iMac on the Apple website, you will find it under the following URL: "http://www.apple.com/imac/." However, you will also find it under the shorter and more memorable URL: "http://www.imac.com." Both URLs go to the same page.

If you are promoting a certain product or offering, publish the specific URL that will bring the reader to the relevant section on the website, rather than the generic homepage. For example, if you are promoting the iMac, you wouldn't point the reader to "http://www.apple.com." Rather, you'd point them to "http://www.imac.com."

CONCLUSION

Few investments in website design are as critical – and as difficult – as planning, testing and implementing a navigation system that's simple, intuitive and comprehensive enough to serve readers. Adhere to basic navigation design principles, the first of which is that you should design navigation from the reader's point of view. Follow standard Web conventions as closely as possible, and make sure your navigation works by testing it at each stage of its development.

Readers like a variety of ways to navigate through a website. Make sure that you include a wide enough range of navigation options to account for different readers' habits and tastes. Think of navigation as a "road sign" system. It's there to point the reader in the right direction.

CONTENT LAYOUT AND DESIGN

9

CONTENT MUST BE READABLE

In the previous two chapters we have concentrated on how best to organize and navigate content. We have examined metadata and classification, search, and navigation – three of the four pillars of information architecture. In this chapter we examine the fourth – layout and design. We have left it for last because its success largely depends on having the other three pillars in place.

Properly laid-out content enhances the reader's experience and ensures that information is communicated efficiently. The best layout for online reading is rarely the same as for paper, because the screen is different to the page and because readers behave differently online.

That said, laying out content still begins and ends with the reader. What you want to achieve is the most "readable" environment for your content. It needs to be understood that reading on a computer screen is more difficult than reading off a printed page. This means that layout on a website must be more simple and straightforward than for print. Visual design should support and enhance the content layout, as well as the presentation of navigation and search.

It is not the objective of Content Critical to go into great detail on how content should be presented. Rather, we would like to illustrate the key issues that should be considered when laying out content.

GENERAL CONTENT LAYOUT CONVENTIONS

The following general conventions apply to content on the Internet:

- For maximum readability, text should be black on a white background (85 percent white is the preferred shading). Short pieces of text which are found on homepages or in the right or left columns of other pages may use different colors, depending on design issues. However, always use strong contrast in color so the text can be as easily read as possible.

- Avoid using italics. Unless a computer screen has a very high resolution, italics can look coarse – as if the word is breaking up. Even with high-resolution screens, italics should be used sparingly. Italics are used sparingly even in print. Never put entire sentences or paragraphs into italics. This is bad style, period.

- Avoid using bold within the body of the text as some readers will mistake bolded text for a link. Even in print, bold is used sparingly, particularly in body text. It looks crude and amateurish, as if the words are shouting for attention.

- Never underline as a reader will think it's a link.

- Choose sans serif fonts if possible, as these use straight lines and are therefore easier to read online. Serif fonts, on the other hand, use a lot of curves, which tend to read poorly on a screen, particularly at smaller font sizes.

- Because it's harder to read text on a screen, avoid using small font sizes. Small quantities of text on homepages can be presented as small as 8-point (-2 in HTML). However, for body text in a document, you shouldn't go lower than 10-point (-1 in HTML).

- Avoid things that move. Scrolling text or animations make it very difficult to read text that is presented close by. While such movement can have some benefit on a homepage, it should be very much avoided in document pages where a lot of reading is being done.

Headings and summaries

Quality headings and summaries are critical to the success of an online publication. There are two basic reasons for this:

- The nature of hypertext is that you "click down" into content. On a homepage, for example, you will invariably find headings and summaries. Done right they act as a "call to action," encouraging you to "click for more."

- Readers consistently use Search to find content they are looking for. The search results page is presented to the reader as a set of headings and summaries. The decision to click or not to click is based on what the reader reads in these headings and summaries.

Most headings and summaries on the Internet are poor. Headings often give you very little clue as to what the document is actually about.

Most headings and summaries you find on the Internet are poor. Headings often give you very little clue as to what the document is actually about. Summaries tend to grab whatever 30 words they can find, regardless of whether they "summarize" the document or not.

If an online publication wishes to increase the chances that its readers will "click for more" it needs to focus on improving the heading and summary writing skills of its authors. Writing first-class headings and summaries is a skill that can take years to acquire. However, most people can be trained to avoid making fundamental mistakes.

Laying out documents

If headings and summaries are the "appetizers" of a website, the document is the "meat." the Web is changing the very nature of how we create and read documents. One of the best ways to illustrate this is to look at how technology has changed the way we create and listen to music.

Some of us will remember the vinyl album. It had 10 or 12 tracks with a total of about 40 minutes of music. This wasn't because artists naturally tended to produce music in such quantities. Rather, it was because a 12-in piece of vinyl could hold only about 40 minutes of music. With the advent of the CD, many albums became longer (55–60 minutes) not because of some increase in creative energy, but rather because CDs could comfortably hold 60 minutes of music.

The Internet is changing the whole concept of the "album" because it is introducing new means of distribution for music. Napster is just one example of how music can now be easily distributed in single-song units. It's easy to imagine that in time artists will have a "song bank" on which fans will be able to pick and choose which tracks they would like to buy, and the "album" may become a relic of history.

The very same process will happen to text-based content. Historically, a significant quantity of such content has been created in long documents (reports, books, manuals, etc.) The print costs of production often encouraged such an approach. It is cheaper to print and distribute one document that is 50 pages long, than to separately print and distribute 10 documents that are five pages long.

That all changes with the Web for the following reasons:

- Distribution costs are close to zero.

- In our attention-deficit environment – especially online – people like to scan-read and prefer smaller and smaller chunks of content.

- Time-to-publish becomes ever more critical for content. Vital content was often held up in traditional print processes until the entire document was ready to be printed.

The result is that, on the Web, documents need to be:

- **short** – overall length needs to be short as do paragraphs. Sub-headings and highlighted sentences should be used to break up the document so it can be more easily scan-read;

- **linked** – rather than waiting for a traditional document of 10 sections to be finished before it is published, it makes sense to publish each section as it is ready, linking one section to another as appropriate;

- **published quickly** – documents should be of a size that they can move quickly through the publishing process, as time-to-publish is becoming as critical to the organization as time-to-market;

- **interactive** – publishing the name of the author with an email address adds credibility and gives the reader the opportunity to respond;

- **dated** – the reader will become tired of out-of-date content on the Web. Having a date at the top of the document quickly establishes its timeliness.

- **clearly marked for copyright** – it's so easy to copy something on the Web, so it's vital that every document contains appropriate copyright information.

It goes without saying that readers are more likely to read content that is specifically written for the Web. However, it is amazing how many organizations shovel their print documents onto the Web in the form of

Microsoft Word or Adobe Acrobat documents. This may be necessary in an intranet environment where a lot of detailed, technical documentation needs to be presented. However, even in these circumstances, clear headings and comprehensive summaries should be provided before the reader is asked to download such files.

When publishing them, the following procedures are recommended:

■ Clearly indicate what type of document it is (Word, PDF, Excel, etc.).

■ State the size of the document.

■ Clearly state whether the reader will require special software to read it.

■ Provide a link to a source for that software, if appropriate.

■ Provide a summary in HTML as to what is in the document.

Laying out forms

Forms are a structured way by which information is gathered from a reader. Forms should be used for the following reasons:

■ In a subscription process where you need to gather information on the subscriber.

■ In a feedback process where the reader wants to send you a request for further information.

■ In a purchase process where the reader wants to purchase a product from the website.

■ In a download process where a reader wants to download software or other content for a trial or test period.

There are a number of key rules that should be followed when creating forms:

■ Gather what is essential. If, for example, an email address is essential for the successful completion of the process, then make that field mandatory, so that the reader cannot complete the form if they have not filled in that field.

■ Gather only what is necessary. Organizations love to gather as much information on their readers as possible. Readers hate giving away

Gather only what is necessary. Readers hate giving away personal information and hate filling out long forms.

personal information and hate filling out long forms. If you make the form too long, people will either not fill it out at all or will skip large chunks of it.

■ Ask questions your readers can and are willing to answer. Not every country has a ZIP code but many forms targeted at international readers demand that a ZIP code be entered. Again, forms, like every other type of content, should be created with the reader in mind.

LAYING OUT EMAIL PUBLICATIONS

Email publications (newsletters) are a highly effective way of keeping your readers regularly informed. They are a must for every Internet publication. (See subscription-based publishing in Chapter 10.) Like all publications, an email newsletter begins by identifying a need that the reader has for content. The publication schedule is important to decide. Once a week is ideal. Of course, you may decide to have an infrequent publication, whereby it is published only when, for example, a new product feature is released.

Keep your newsletter short and snappy. Write punchy summaries and link back to the full document on the website. Keep all articles at less than 600 words if possible, as few people will read them if they are much longer. When putting together email publications keep the following in mind:

■ While you can create your newsletter using HTML, plain text is generally best. If you do offer HTML, offer a plain text version as well, as some email programs cannot read HTML.

■ Have a line length of between 60 and 70 characters, as some email programs break up lines longer than that.

■ Never send a newsletter as an attachment to an email, as, for example, a Microsoft Word document.

■ The subject line of the email should contain a heading describing the current issue.

- Always date the publication.

- Make sure you have lots of appropriate links back to the website. When creating a link, always use the full address (http://www.) as some email systems will not turn it into a link otherwise.

- When dealing with an email address, use the "mailto:" function in front of the address, as this links the address to the reader's email program. For example, mailto:peter@abc.com.

- Clearly differentiate advertisements from the rest of the content.

- The footer information of the publication should contain subscription and unsubscription details, contact details, etc.

GRAPHIC WEB DESIGN

Many traditional graphic designers dislike the Web, because they must "dumb down" their work to fit into a limited visual medium. To many designers the promise of broadband is like the promise of heaven to a Christian. Unfortunately a great many Christians may see heaven before designers will see broadband for the masses.

The fact is that those who are waiting for broadband are missing the point. For essential functions such as the delivery of text-based content there is ample bandwidth already. Instead of trying to turn the Web into a high-visual medium, we badly need a new breed of designer – a Web-publishing designer.

Before looking at principles of graphic Web design, it's important to understand that the role of Web page design is to present to the reader Web pages that are readable, intuitive, easy to navigate, and visually pleasing, in that order. In approaching Web page design it is worthwhile reiterating fundamental Web publishing principles:

- The reader is king.

- Know the reader.

- Help the reader to find the content they want quickly.

- Guide the reader.

- Deliver up to date, accurate, relevant and straightforward content.
- Present the content in an inviting, Web-tailored format.
- Respect the reader.
- Invite the reader to interact.
- Write for the Web.
- Keep it simple.

Keeping the above principles in mind, the purpose of graphic Web design is to:

- create simple, easy-to-read pages. Study after study shows that people come to the Internet fundamentally to find information. A four-year study by the Poynter Institute clearly showed that the first thing people do when they visit a website is read;
- create a consistent environment. All pages should be laid out in a consistent manner;
- create a highly navigable environment. It should be clear to the reader how to navigate and search the website;
- establish a sense of style. There are a lot of elements at play on any one web page. Good design makes it all look coherent;
- establish a sense of balance between the need to deliver a content-rich, fast-downloading, highly functional website, and one that is pleasing to look at, incorporates organizational branding requirements, and is easy to navigate;
- make sure that pages are "light" so they will download quickly. There is a rule in the industry that the average reader will wait no longer than 10 seconds for a page to download before giving up. (Some estimate that many readers will wait no longer than four seconds.) Measure bandwidth availability by its weakest link;
- get results by following the motto – keep it simple, functional and quick to download.

General design conventions

At all costs avoid "intro" or "splash" pages. They are a total waste of time.

- Scrolling is preferable to clicking. The over-riding concern of the reader is to find the content they want quickly. In that sense they prefer a "cluttered" page that allows them to navigate or search quickly for the content they need rather than an elegant, spare page that requires them to click several times to get to content. At all costs avoid "intro" or "splash" pages. They are a total waste of time. (The exception is for language navigation. See Chapter 8.)

- Avoid animations except for animated banner ads or ticker-tape functions, as they will distract the reader away from content. Peripheral vision is especially sensitive to animation, which therefore should be avoided particularly at the edges of the screen. Banner ads should rotate the animation once or twice and then stop. The reader should be able to turn on and off ticker tapes.

- Avoid using frames for the following reasons:
  - Readers are not used to them; the vast majority of websites do not use frames.
  - They are generally slower to render in most browsers.
  - They cannot be bookmarked.
  - It can be extremely frustrating for the reader to leave a framed website with one of the frames going with them.

- Keep graphics small in terms of file size and physical size. There is no bigger turn-off on the Web than to arrive at a homepage and have to watch a big graphic slowly downloading.

- Adhere to the navigation design principles as outlined in Chapter 8.

- The ideal layout that will present the most content in the most readable format on a Web page is the three-column layout. As a rough guide the left and right columns should take up a quarter each of the page width, with the center column taking up half of the width.

Mastheads: the importance of slim design

When average readers load up a web page on an average small computer screen, the organization in question wants to present them with the widest and most appealing range of content possible. To do this it needs to maximize the amount of space it has available for presenting this content.

The masthead is the top of the page area on the website. It generally contains the organization logo and other graphic elements. Traditional designers might describe the masthead as a "branding space." Unfortunately, many designers misunderstand how branding actually works on the Web. If you want to turn your reader off your brand then present them with a masthead that takes up half the page and takes half a minute to download. Readers rightly view such branding approaches as amateurish and time-wasting.

In the attention-deficit economy brands scream for attention. On the Web, brands are supposed to *give* attention. The difference is that of night and day. Walk into a newsagent, and 200 brands call out to you – colorful, teasing, provocative. They yearn for you to pick them up.

What's the first thing you do when you want to go to a website? You type in the brand! (www.yahoo.com, www.microsoft.com, www.napster.com, www.ibm.com, www.aol.com, www.ebay.com.) The brand has already got your attention. You go to the website to do something. The last thing you want is a big swirling logo. Go to the above websites. See how little space on the page the logo takes up.

Therefore, it's important to keep your masthead slim (ideally no more than 70–90 pixels deep), so that on the rest of the screen you can present as much content and as many navigation options to the reader as possible. The masthead should contain:

- the logo of the organization, the name of the department, subdivision, etc;

- the global navigation;

- e-commerce navigation, if appropriate;

- and, ideally, the search facility.

FIGURE 9.1

Footers: don't forget essential information

Footers refer to essential bottom-of-page information. Every page should have a footer that is clearly delineated. This footer should contain:

- global navigation as text;
- e-commerce navigation as text (if available).
- contact information, including email, phone, fax, and geographical address. If the organization has more than two addresses, a contact link can be used instead;
- a "Terms of Use" link. (See copyright and legal issues in Chapter 5);
- a "Privacy Policy" link;
- a "Copyright © 1995–2001 Example Company. All rights reserved" link.

FIGURE 9.2

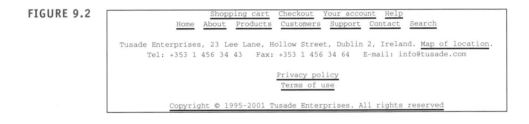

ACCESSIBILITY

It's important to have a view about how accessible the website needs to be for people with visual and other impairments. A balance needs to be achieved between making the website very accessible and limiting what you can do with it, and adding substantial extra cost to developing it.

Making a website accessible generally improves the usability of the site for everyone.

In an increasing number of countries adherence to certain accessibility standards is demanded by law. However, accessibility standards are not simply about the law; they often make very good sense from a design point of view. Making a website accessible generally improves the usability of the site for everyone.

It is often not practical to have your website meet every single accessibility standard. You should prioritize them and aim to have at least the homepage and other highly trafficked pages accessible. There are a number of organizations that provide detailed accessibility standards, including the W3C guidelines on Web Content Accessibility (www.w3.org/TR/WCAG10/) and the Electronic and Information Technology Accessibility Standards of the US Architectural And Transportation Barriers Compliance Board (www.access-board.gov/sec508/508standards.htm).

Key accessibility issues to look out for include:

- Proper use of mark-up – make sure the HTML code is written correctly. Don't take short cuts.
- Images – provide ALT text with all images.
- Design – make sure there is strong contrast between the foreground and background design.
- Navigation – navigation design in a consistent manner.
- Screen movement – avoid undue movement on the screen.
- Technologies – avoid using non-standard technologies that require viewing with either plug-ins or stand-alone applications.
- Tables – mark up tables correctly, and clearly identify row and column headers.
- Applets and scripts – ensure that pages can still be used even if they are viewed with a browser that does not support scripts, applets or other programatic objects.
- Frames – frames are not recommended.
- Multimedia – provide an audio summary of the main points of the visual multimedia presentation.
- Forms – allow people filling out forms using assistive technology to access all the information, field elements and functionality required for completion and submission of the form, including all directions and cues.

CONCLUSION

A website is there to deliver content to the reader with a minimum of obstacles and distractions. By applying consistent standards of layout and design that put the reader first and that recognize the Web's limitations and advantages, you can vastly increase the usefulness and efficiency of your website.

Website design is about designing for the reader. It's about simplicity and functionality. Websites should be as accessible as possible to people with disabilities. Remember, when it comes to text-based content, the style is invariably found in the text itself, not in the visuals that surround the text.

SPECIAL TOPICS IN WEB PUBLISHING

10

The Holy Grail of every publisher is to get subscribers. In this chapter we look at subscription-based publishing from a Web perspective. The greatly enhanced ability of the Web to facilitate reader interaction and feedback is also explored. We also examine how promotion is an even more important activity for a Web publisher than for a traditional publisher. Finally, we will explore issues relating to the measurement of a Web publication's performance.

SUBSCRIPTION-BASED PUBLISHING

A website is a "pull" medium. What this means is that a website must constantly be attracting readers. In an attention-deficit economy, this is no easy task. A fundamental objective of any website should therefore be to "push" content to its readers. What this means is that after the reader has signed up to a subscription service, they will get content sent to them, generally by email. This is subscription-based publishing. (Another form of subscription service is to offer readers access to a restricted part of a website.) To subscribe to such a service the reader must give personal information (such as an email address) and/or agree to make a payment.

The cornerstone of subscription-based publishing is an "opt-in" approach. Never send content to people who have not specifically requested it, as this will be regarded as spam. Spam is unsolicited email, and is a guaranteed way to annoy a great many people. (Legislation is pending in a number of countries that will make spam illegal.)

When asking readers to subscribe to something, provide them with all the relevant information they require.

When asking readers to subscribe to something, provide them with all the relevant information they require. This includes the scope of the publication, whether or not it is free, the publication schedule, how to subscribe and unsubscribe. State clearly to readers the privacy policy, and how their personal information will be treated.

It's very important to keep the subscription and unsubscription processes as simple as possible. People hate filling out forms and if you ask for too much information many won't subscribe. When a request for subscription arrives, verify it by sending a message to the email address supplied as this will ensure that someone has not been maliciously subscribed. When the subscription is found to be correct, send the new subscriber a confirmation message which should include all essential details about the service. These details will include subscription and unsubscription information, as well as the address the person subscribed with.

Subscriber lists require ongoing management. People will inevitably have problems unsubscribing. Many will change their email address or their job, and forget to unsubscribe. Be prepared to allocate some time every week to make sure the subscriber list is kept up to date.

As we have already outlined, privacy is a key issue on the Internet. At all costs make sure that your subscription list is well protected. There have been a number of PR disasters relating to stolen subscriber lists. Make sure and back-up your list. It's a very valuable asset and you don't want to lose it.

Managing passwords

If a subscription process is Web-based, some sort of password system will be required. Passwords are the bane of most people's lives. Therefore it is important to keep the password process as simple and user-friendly as possible. On a general point, if your website has a password-protected section, clearly flag it to the reader.

Here are some recommendations when developing a password system:

- Practically all password systems require username information. If possible, allow the subscriber to choose their own username as they're more likely to remember it.

- A critical piece of information to obtain is the prospective subscriber's email address. Use error-checking in the email address field so, if they forget to include the @ symbol, for example, this is flagged.

- The password field itself should have a minimum of six characters. Advise the reader not to choose a common word, and, if possible, to use a mix of letters and numbers. Always provide a second password field for verification purposes.

- Once the subscriber has received their password, it's very helpful to offer them the option of saving that password so they won't have to enter it every time they visit the website. This can be done with cookie software.

READER INTERACTION AND FEEDBACK

As outlined in previous chapters it is critical that the organization makes it possible for the reader to interact. It should consider the following issues when developing a policy for reader interaction:

- How this is to be channeled. Who do sales queries go to? Or support queries?

- The response schedule for interaction. A key way a reader judges a website is by how quickly and professionally it responds to a query. If a sales query is received, how quickly will the reader get a response – 24 hours? 12 hours? 1 hour? Is there a need for auto-responders in some situations?

- The variety of interaction that is to be encouraged. Sales and support queries are a must. However, it is also good policy on the Internet that authors of content provide email contact details with each document they publish, to allow the reader to get in touch with questions or feedback.

- The type of interaction facilities – email, online chat, telephone and fax, geographical address, ring-back, etc.

- Quality control – how does the organization measure the quality of response the reader is receiving? Is there a need to cc all replies to the editor?

On every page of a website there should be a "Contact" link, found in the global navigation. This should be obvious, but a surprising number of websites either don't have comprehensive contact details, or else hide them in some obscure place. We recommend that a contact link be placed in the global navigation and in the footer.

The contact link should contain email contact information, telephone and fax information, geographical address of offices and a how-to-get-here map of each location. The email contact facility should ideally link through to a form, as should all other email contact links. This protects against spammers "harvesting" email addresses from the website. It also ensures more structured communication from the reader.

It should be policy that all contact with the organization should get at least an initial response within one working day. This needs to be tracked and measured. Where an email contact has been sent by the reader, it is recommended that an auto-response mechanism be used that will inform them that their email has been received and will be acted upon within a specified period. Advanced contact facilities such as call-back are encouraged, particularly where there is a need for the organization to respond to the reader quickly.

Launching a website is a bit like building a store at the North Pole. Nobody knows you're there unless you actively promote the site. There are millions of websites; how is yours going to stand out?

Launching a website is a bit like building a store at the North Pole. Nobody knows you're there unless you actively promote the site. There are millions of websites; how is yours going to stand out? Even if you're developing an intranet you can't automatically assume that the staff will be poised over their keyboards waiting for the site to launch. Accept that a website is at heart a publication, and that readers are its lifeblood. It doesn't matter how good your content is – if you don't have readers you're going nowhere.

Promotion is even more important online than offline. People say that the Web has zero distribution costs; that's because it has zero distribution! That's a double-edged sword from a promotion point of view. Traditional publishers use distribution to promote their publication as much as to distribute it. Getting your newspaper, magazine or book displayed prominently on a news-stand or in a bookshop will have a significant impact on the number of copies you will sell. Because a website has such little visibility, promotion becomes a critical activity that should really be carried out each day. Here we examine various ways you can actively promote your website.

Use your homepage

The days of vast promotion budgets for websites are gone. However, there are a lot of simple things that a Web publication can do to ensure that as many people as possible know about it and visit. For starters, look at your homepage as a promotion tool. Its job is to take the most interesting and important content and polish it up into short, sharp summaries that make the reader want to click for more.

A perfect example of this promotional approach can be found at the Microsoft homepage. Microsoft allocates more than half of its page to breezy promotional content. On June 3, 2001, for example, the story of the day was, "Office XP is here." The other stories included, "May the source be with you" (a feature promoting XML); "Build a retail site" (a feature promoting .NET); and "Deploy Active Directory." All these were calls to action, designed to get the reader to click deeper into the website.

FIGURE 10.1

Get links

Think about links like a road network. The more links you have to your website, the more roads that lead to it, and therefore the more ways your reader has to get to it. Done right, linking is very powerful. It's like embedded "word-of-mouth." The question is, how do you get links? For starters, you need to have a reason for another website to link to you, and that involves having quality content that may be of interest to that website's readers.

A strategy for getting links is to use a reciprocal linking approach. This involves offering to link to another website if they link to you. (If for whatever reason you are linking to another website always ask for a link back.) The problem here is that you don't want a big links section on your website, as it will look cumbersome and, of course, invites readers to leave.

Links don't grow on trees. They have to be worked at. You carefully need to choose websites that attract your target readership, and communicate with the people who run them about getting links established.

Affiliate programs work well from a linking point of view. Amazon, for example, has millions of other websites that link to it through its affiliate program. The Google search engine has an innovative link-type strategy whereby you download a small Google search function that integrates into your browser. Some websites have initiated awards/review programs whereby the reviewed websites download an icon that links back to the reviewer's website.

Get registered (at your friendly search engine)

It goes without saying that every website (excluding intranets and extranets) should register with the major search engines. There are hundreds of search engines and directories but only a small number that matter. The most important of these are Yahoo, Google and Alta Vista. (Other important ones are: Microsoft Network, Excite, Lycos, Go, HotBot, All The Web, Direct Hit, Look Smart and Northern Light.) However, there may be some specialist websites that deal with your specific sector, so make sure you register with them.

Search engine registration is an inexact science and the rules keep changing. After your initial registration you should allocate some time at least once a month to making sure that your website remains well-registered. Be careful not to abuse the search engine registration process by submitting keywords that are popular but not really relevant to your website. (An increasing number of search engines are now charging a registration fee.)

Other promotion devices

Banner advertising may be losing its effectiveness but it can still be a useful internal tool for pointing readers to important content on your website. For example, in a large intranet you might want to promote a change in HR policy. A simple ad could be developed and deployed throughout the site with the banner ad system.

Competitions are always a useful way of attracting attention, particularly if you're offering something for free. If you have an email newsletter, a short, snappy ad that promotes important elements on the website can be used. Email signatures can help as promotional tools. For example, when Andersen Consulting changed its name to Accenture, every member of staff had an email signature that told the reader of the change. (Keep such signatures short – five lines or less.) If you're promoting an intranet why not create simple flyers or posters?

FIGURE 10.2

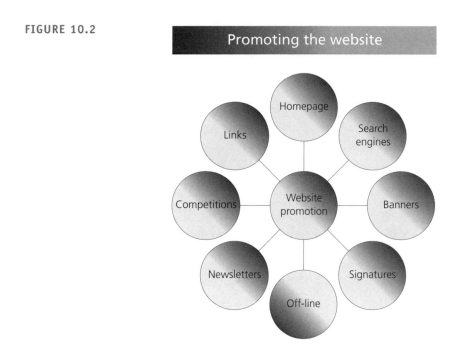

Promoting the website

Traditionally, it has been very difficult to measure a publication's performance, except in the crudest of ways – it sold or it didn't. Within a particular publication it was quite difficult to track which articles were read the most and which the least. The Web provides much better tools for measuring the performance of content.

Decide what is really important. Leave the rest aside, or it will get in the way.

Unfortunately, the Web offers so many ways to measure things that it can throw up mountains of largely unusable data. On a day-to-day basis, with everyone being so busy, there is often little time or inclination to decipher, let alone act on, this data. This is something to watch out for when designing a measurement system for a Web publication. Decide what is really important and measure it. Leave the rest aside, or it will get in the way.

There are three key things you need to measure for any website:

- The number of readers who visit and their behavior.
- The performance of the people who create, edit and publish content on the website.
- The performance of the technology and software that runs the website.

From a reader perspective the key things you need to measure over a defined period (weekly, monthly) include:

- How many people came to the website?
- How many of these were unique, as against repeat visitors?
- How many page impressions/views were there?
- What were the 10 most popular parts of the website?
- How many new subscribers were there to the subscription services? How many were lost?

For a publishing organization, the key things to measure are:

- How many new documents were published on the website?
- Are documents getting published quickly enough?
- Is the publication schedule being adhered to?
- How well did a sample of these documents reflect the publication scope and tone?
- Is out-of-date content being removed quickly?
- Is the metadata on new documents published of a sufficient quality?
- Are the interactive elements being moderated properly?
- Are reader queries being responded to quickly?

Technology and software measurables will include the following:

- Are pages downloading quickly?
- Is downtime being kept to a minimum?
- Are the publishing processes working efficiently?

CONCLUSION

The Web is a pull medium and that makes it difficult to attract readers and keep them coming back. A quality subscription-based publishing approach can help solve this problem. The Web offers the potential for strong interactivity, but if there isn't a policy in place it won't happen.

Remember, your website starts at the North Pole of reader recognition, so actively promoting your content is critical. Finally, the Web offers a wide range of tools with which to measure performance. Decide on what is really important to measure. Otherwise, you risk getting drowned in data.

THE PUBLISHING TEAM

11

Because many organizations have failed to understand that the Web is a publishing medium, they have failed to create the kinds of internal organizations needed to produce a quality publication. Too often, organizations have approached the job of designing, creating and publishing a website as though they were producing a brochure – a one-off job that merely requires some meetings with designers and software engineers, a little teamwork, and a big effort to get the website up and running. Then everyone can go back to business as usual.

The result of that kind of thinking is the plethora of poorly thought-out, static and unreadable sites on the Web today, most of which fall far short of fulfilling their organizations' strategies. As we've seen in the preceding 10 chapters, the issues involved in producing a sophisticated, reader-friendly website – from creating content to editing, managing and publishing it – are many and complex. Unless the organization creates, staffs and funds the right kind of team to publish its content, its website will not succeed.

PUBLISHING TEAM: ROLES AND ORGANIZATION

Given the vast range of websites – from small ones that publish limited amounts of content infrequently with a single member of staff, to large, high-volume websites with dozens of dedicated employees – specifying detailed organizational hierarchies for Web publishers is beyond the scope of this book. Instead, we have isolated the key functions that need to be carried out by *any* website, and will specify the roles, necessary skills and responsibilities for each. These are:

- publisher;
- managing editor;
- editor;
- copyeditor;
- writer/author;

- contributor;
- moderator;
- information architect;
- HTML coder;
- graphic designer;
- systems administrator/junior programer;
- usability expert;
- marketing executive.

In a small organization many of these roles may be filled by one person; for a large website each will be performed by one or more people. You'll notice that we haven't included the role of Webmaster. This catch-all job title, which emerged with the early Web, is so poorly defined as to be virtually meaningless. In some organizations the Webmaster is the top technology person, in others the top editorial person. In too many, the Webmaster is merely a junior person who copyedits and knows a little HTML. We recommend sticking with job titles that reflect their function in an accurate way. However, the important thing is not so much the job title used but rather the awareness that the person who manages and drives the website should understand and champion content first and technology and graphical design second.

As outlined in Chapter 6, Editing Content, editorial responsibility for the publication should ideally be vested in one person, whom we identify as the managing editor. However, overall responsibility for the publication is shared between the managing editor and the publisher, who is responsible for the "business side" of the website. This involves everything from selling advertising (if the site generates revenue that way) to arranging for the technical resources to publish the content.

There will always be a certain conflict between the editorial and business sides. Editors and authors will want more content, more interactivity and more resources in general. The publisher will have technical restrictions and financial pressures. In commercial publishing this conflict can be intense. Indeed, the term "church and state" is often used in journalism to indicate the need for a clear line of demarcation between the publisher (who is focussed on the business) and the editor (who is focussed on editorial quality).

We will not be dealing in great detail with the role of the publisher, since it is most applicable to commercial publishing entities such as online magazines and news providers, and is therefore fairly specialized. But we will outline the publisher's responsibilities, since they exist in any publishing organization. What is essential is that the managing editor and publisher have a mutual understanding of the organization's overall Web strategy and its resources.

Also as outlined in Chapter 6, an editorial board, comprised of representatives of different constituencies within the organization, may decide strategic and policy issues that the managing editor and the publisher will implement. Both individuals should report to such a board, or to the same individual corporate manager.

Team members

Publisher

The role of publisher involves responsibility for all the commercial, accounting and promotional aspects of the publication. In smaller commercial publications, or where the commercial and promotional aspects of the publication are not substantial (as in an intranet), the publisher's responsibilities may be carried out by the managing editor. Publishers tend to be necessary only where the publication is strictly commercially-driven – where it needs to turn a profit as a result of its operations.

The publisher must have a broad knowledge of publishing, strong commercial and financial skills, and a keen ability to promote a publication and to sell advertising. It is also desirable that the publisher has experience in establishing commercial partnerships.

The publisher's primary responsibility is to ensure that the publication is a commercial success, while managing costs and promoting the publication.

Managing editor

The managing editor is responsible for the timeliness and quality of the website's content, and for the quality and efficiency of the editorial processes. They oversee the website's overall editorial strategy and policies, approval policies, and content commission and acquisition processes. The managing editor also gives progress reports and analysis on the website to the organization.

The managing editor must have an in-depth knowledge of the organization's publishing strategy, editorial policies and approval processes. The managing editor should have extensive experience with off-line and online publications, and should be familiar with all the jobs involved in creating, editing and publishing content within the organization. Ideally, the managing editor should be skilled at most of these jobs, and should have substantial experience – and highly developed skills – in editing and writing.

The two most important responsibilities of the managing editor are to motivate authors to create quality content, and to understand the readers' needs. Ability to fully interact with and motivate readers and to communicate with them in a positive way is essential, as is the ability to manage editors and authors. The managing editor must have a profound understanding of the organization's business and the ability to evolve the publishing strategy.

Specific responsibilities of the managing editor include:

Managing content

The managing editor is the key person choosing the feature content for the homepage. This should be done in consultation with the other editors, and may also require input from the editorial board, if one exists, or from key members of the organization's senior management. The importance of selecting homepage content can't be over-emphasized – an organization's homepage is its most important presence on the Web. It is what most readers will see first, and what most readers will bookmark. In print publishing, decisions about what goes on the front page of a newspaper or on the cover of a magazine are made at the highest levels. The homepage of a website is no less important. The most senior executives of an organization should know what's on their website's homepage and why it's there.

> **The most senior executives of an organization should know what's on their website's homepage and why it's there.**

The overall quality of the website's content and the way it is featured and displayed is also the managing editor's responsibility.

Managing the editorial process

The managing editor must set the publication schedule and ensure that it is met so that the website is published every day (or other interval) at the same time. The managing editor is responsible for all the content workflows that have been detailed in earlier chapters, including those for creating, commissioning, acquiring, contributing, editing, correcting and deleting content.

Managing the staff

The managing editor should be in charge of hiring, training, motivating, assessing and – when necessary – disciplining the editorial staff. An important part of this job is to establish and manage content reward and motivation schemes. Identifying training needs and implementing appropriate training courses is also important.

Championing the reader

Everything the managing editor does should be done with the reader in mind. Specific responsibilities related to readers include managing and encouraging reader interactivity, responding to readers' queries, establishing and monitoring response times to reader queries, initiating periodic reader surveys, and actively encouraging reader feedback.

Championing the website

The managing editor should be the champion for the website within the larger organization. This involves attending wider management meetings, promoting the website to a wider management audience, and seeking feedback from key constituencies within the organization. The managing editor should also provide feedback to management about proposed changes in strategy.

Monitoring, reviewing and reporting

This is one of the most essential functions in ensuring the continuing success of the website. The managing editor should initiate periodic reviews of the site's content, design and functionality, and create a continuing plan for the reporting and analysis process. Other tasks include monitoring reader usage, content analysis and publishing performance, and ensuring that the classification and navigation systems evolve as the site grows.

Editor

Editors are the key members of the team charged with ensuring the quality of the publication. The editor should be empowered to commission content from writers (or to acquire it from third parties), and should have plenty of latitude in deciding basic questions of appropriateness, length, tone and quality of pieces of content. The editor determines whether an article should be rewritten. They should also be responsible for arranging for any accompanying graphics.

The skills editors should possess a subset of the skills required by the managing editor. The job requires significant experience with print and online publications, an understanding of the organization's publishing goals and strategy, and sufficient judgment and people skills to ensure the best work of writers and contributors. The editor must have very strong word skills, including the ability to rearrange and rewrite content swiftly and efficiently if needs be.

The editors' skills must be enough to allow them to: carry out general editing; write effective headings, summaries and subheadings; copyedit and proofread; implement usability guidelines; and understand and interact with readers.

Ideally, editors should also possess two special talents. First, is the ability and willingness to overcome their own egos. The best editors improve the quality of their writers' content without imposing their own tastes on it. And since much of their work is invisible to those outside the organization, editors must be willing to sacrifice the kind of public attention that writers often enjoy.

Second is the ability to deal empathetically with writers. Writing is difficult, and most writers are sensitive about their work. Editors must be able to request and suggest changes when needed, and to ask sometimes that content be entirely rewritten. They must also be able to reject content. To be able to do this graciously is a rare skill.

The editor's specific responsibilities include:

Commissioning and acquiring content

The editor creates and oversees the calendar of events for their area, and commissions content. This includes identifying and filling gaps in content, developing cost/benefit for acquiring content, and overseeing its flow. The editor must be familiar with all potential sources of content, both inside the organization and outside, and should be in charge of the payment process.

Editing content

The editor selects content and checks it over, and reviews classification and metadata, before forwarding it to others (to the legal department, for instance) for further review. The editor may edit, cut, rewrite or rephrase content, or return it to writers and contributors for further work. The editor also reviews, corrects and deletes published content as necessary.

Managing the publication process

The editor creates and maintains document templates; identifies important content and rearranges Web pages to highlight it; previews completed content and moves it to the next stage, copyediting. The editor also checks that metadata is being properly completed.

Managing writers and readers

Day-to-day management of content reward and motivation schemes and of training courses is the editor's responsibility. The manager also manages and encourages reader interactivity, and ensures that search engine registration processes and other promotional activities are being carried out effectively (if there is no publisher).

Copyeditor

Copyeditors are responsible for ensuring that content contains correct grammar and spelling and adheres to house style. They also check for errors in structure and facts, ensuring that the end product is well-written, consistently styled and error-free.

The skills and talents required of copyeditors include an ability to edit written material so it is fluent and logical, a highly developed critical sense, a sharp eye for detail, structure and style, and an ability to communicate clearly and constructively with a wide range of people. In a Web environment, the copyeditor has a new responsibility – to ensure that metadata has been entered correctly for each document.

Author/writer

Writers create content. They may work individually or collaborate with other authors. Documents are created using a word-processing package, presentation package, or by entering text directly into document templates provided by the organization's content management application.

The writer's skills, first and foremost, are an ability to write, an enthusiasm for language and writing, and curiosity. Writers must be knowledgeable about the organization's editorial policies, adept at conducting research, and be expert in their particular field. They must also be capable of working within a team and of interacting with readers.

The writer's specific responsibilities include suggesting content ideas, creating quality content that adheres to the organization's style and tone, and reworking content as required.

Contributor

The contributor submits content to the system for publication. In contributing a document, the contributor ensures that the classification, keywords and other metadata are entered. They may also be required to write headings and summaries for the content. Required skills include an ability to carry out research, expertise in their particular field, knowledge of the classification system in use, and familiarity with keyword selection, summary creation and heading creation.

Specific responsibilities include classifying content, specifying metadata, writing headings and summaries, requesting new classifications, requesting improvements to the document templates and the contribution workflow process.

Moderator

The role of the moderator of a discussion board or chat room is about facilitating productive "conversations." In a nutshell, the moderator welcomes newcomers, tries to keep the conversations reasonably on track, and carries out basic housekeeping so there isn't too much clutter and confusion – pruning back the old, extinct discussions like dead tree branches and filtering out inappropriate messages. The moderator maintains a degree of order, blowing the whistle when people argue too heatedly or post inappropriate material.

Skills required of the moderator include patience and a sense of humor, the talents of a natural conversationalist – the life and soul of the party, the one everybody turns to for help – and leadership. The moderator should have reasonable experience of discussion boards, online chat and mailing lists, and expertise and an interest in the content area.

Specific responsibilities of the moderator include facilitating and leading discussions, keeping the discussions "on track," and asking questions of members of the online community to promote discussion; archiving discussions; deleting and adding subscribers to mailing lists; filtering messages to decide which are on-topic; editing and formatting posts, deleting defamatory messages and spam; and marketing and explaining the online community to potential subscribers.

Information architect

Information architects must balance two basic functions. First, they need to create a design that organizes content in a way that meets the internal needs of the organization. The design must be logical and user-friendly, so those contributing content can do so easily and efficiently. To achieve this the architect must understand organization culture and internal "politics." There is often a conflict between logical information architecture and architecture that is politically acceptable. The information architect has the challenging job of balancing these, or at least providing the managing editor with the appropriate arguments with which to push for a particular position.

The second – and what should be the more important – function of the architect is to create an architecture that provides the easiest way for the reader to find and read content. Information architects are needed most in the initial design of the website, though they are also ideally suited to run the production side of the publication as they will have an intimate knowledge of all aspects of how it has been put together.

Information architecture is an emerging discipline and the skills, roles and responsibilities of the information architect are therefore ill-defined. Universities are only beginning to develop courses for this field, though we should see rapid advances considering there is such a need for this skill on any website with a reasonable quantity of content.

The most important skill an information architect requires is the ability to develop proper metadata designs. Classification design is central here, as is the design of the document templates. Metadata is directly linked to the design of search, and the architect must have an excellent grasp of how to create a search function that is simple to use, yet powerful.

Navigation is at the heart of information architecture and the architect must have a keen understanding of navigation design and know when and how to implement various navigation options.

The information architect needs to be skilled in laying out content to allow for optimal readability. This is linked with the look and feel of the website, which they should consider with input from the graphic designer. They need to be skilled in HTML and know how to code pages that are fast to download. Information architecture is intertwined with usability and the architect should either have a background in usability design, or should be able to work hand-in-hand with a usability expert. Among other things, expertise in accessibility design will be required.

Information architects should have a thorough understanding of the software required to run the publication, and be able to advise the managing editor on various software options. They must know about content management applications; subscription-based publishing software; website log software; personalization software; online community software (chat, discussion boards and email mailing lists).

Specific responsibilities of the information architect include overall charge of the architecture of the website; design and management of the metadata, classification, search and navigation; layout and design of the site; the quality of the HTML, and that pages download quickly; usability and accessibility; choice and management of software for managing content, subscription and logging.

HTML coder

HTML coders write the HTML for the website and are often responsible for putting the pages together, under the direction of the information architect. They need to have an excellent understanding of HTML and should have a keen awareness of download and accessibility issues. The importance of HTML coders may depend on the type of content management software being used.

Systems administrator/junior programmer

While the primary focus of any website should be on the content and reader, there is no doubt that there are numerous technical issues involved as well. Websites often suffer because they have not allocated resources to the various technical issues that crop up each day.

Websites often suffer because they have not allocated resources to the various technical issues that crop up each day.

The systems administrator maintains the Web-publishing system once it has been set up. They are also responsible for the network, hosting, servers and other related equipment. Ideally, they should be able to carry out junior programing duties.

Skills required include broad IT and network ability, knowledge of the content management software, the classification system and the work-flow process. When the initial system is installed it is likely that quite an amount of programing will be involved. This will likely be carried out from the IT department or externally. However, there are always small programing jobs that crop up as the system evolves, and it is very helpful if the systems administrator has a basic understanding of programing.

Specific responsibilities include maintaining the network and servers; system back-up; testing page download speeds; basic programing; and providing general support to the information architect.

Graphic designer

The unfortunate graphic designer gets squeezed when it comes to Web design. Because of limited bandwidth, small screens and poor resolution, graphic designers have a more limited role than they would if designing a brochure or magazine.

Graphic designers can report to the information architect or editor, depending on the size of the team. They need to be skilled in graphic design, with a particular talent for creating the most elegant image that is the smallest file size possible. They are responsible for all graphics and images on the website, and should make sure they get plenty of feedback on the look and feel of the site.

Usability expert

Often referred to as a usability engineer, the usability expert is a specialist who ensures that all aspects of the website are easy to use. They support the information architect and are most used in the initial design of the website, and when new elements are added. The usability expert is particularly valu-able at times when the reader is expected to go through a process such as purchasing a product, filling out a form, or using the search function.

Marketing executive

The marketing executive is responsible for the marketing and promotion of the website, as well as ongoing analysis of the log data to decipher reader trends. The Web-specific skills they should possess include those involving search engine registration, promotional linking and log analysis.

FIGURE 11.1

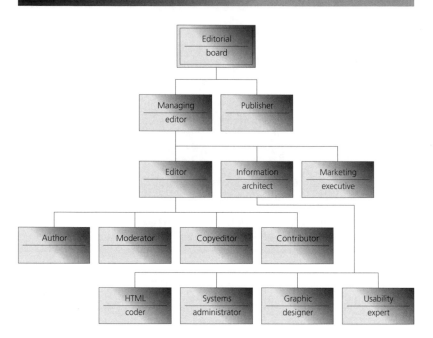

Training

It is important that people involved in the publishing process have the appropriate skills. The two types of publishing skills required are:

- the ability to use the content management software and related software. Some up-front training will inevitably be required here. Without training employees may become inefficient, and mistakes may be made.

- online publishing ability such as writing and editing. It's obvious but true that someone will read and understand well-written content faster than poorly-written content. It should also be understood that writing for the Web requires a different set of skills than writing for other media. To ensure quality content is being produced for the Web, training in online publishing skills is advised.

A policy must be established on how much time is to be spent in training editors, contributors and authors on content management software. The less training, the more likely that mistakes will be made.

A policy should also be set out with regard to whether the organization will promote and fund the training of staff in publishing skills. Without an understanding of the skills required, the quality of content is likely to suffer.

We recommend that all members of the publishing team should receive at least some training on the content management software. Authors and editors should be given the opportunity to have at least 10 hours' training per year on Web-editing and writing skills.

CONCLUSION

The most expensive, technically advanced and glitzy website will fail to meet the organization's goals unless the publishing team is well planned, well organized, motivated and skilled. Every member of the team fulfills an essential role in communicating the website's content. The following extract from the October 2000 issue of Publish magazine sums it up:

"So what does it take to become a great communicator, to utilize Internet technologies to their fullest? It takes a team devoted day in and day out to the company's Internet communication plans, knowing that every word, every graphic, every nuance has to convey exactly the right message to potential customers visiting the company's site. Each member of this team is strategically involved in every level of planning, from marketing and content development to site design and technology implementation."

THE FIVE-STAGE PUBLISHING STRATEGY APPROACH

12

This book has sought to explain the importance of content in the successful operation of a modern organization. Its main theme has been that you treat content as a high-value asset, not as a commodity, as it is being treated by many organizations.

Treating content as a high-value asset requires a publishing approach. This book has sought to outline the key processes and activities involved in publishing content on the Internet.

This chapter develops a five-stage publishing strategy approach which will allow a manager to take the learning developed so far and apply it in a methodical manner to develop a publishing strategy that is practical and workable.

Before embarking on the development of a publishing strategy the organization needs to be cognizant of the core business case. The full business case cannot be developed until a number of the steps in this process have been carried out. However, from the very start you need to outline what you feel the basic business case is.

The business case for a manufacturer could be set out as follows:

- Getting more of the right content to sales reps on time will help them close more sales faster.

- Making sure that there is quality content available on products will help customers and support the sales process. It will also cut costs by reducing the number and length of calls to the telesales departments, while increasing the number of customers converted by telesales.

- Having comprehensive content on product development will improve product development time. It will also facilitate greater collaboration and more idea generation.

- Enabling customers to engage more fully with the organization through interactive and online community activities will make for more satisfied customers and for better feedback to product development, which will ensure that new products better match customer needs.

- Having quality content that is updated regularly, with the out-of-date content removed, will make the organization more efficient, and will portray a positive image to all stakeholders.

Of course, every organization wants all these things. The problem is that quality content takes time, effort and money to create, edit and publish. It will most likely require a raft of new processes and new technology. More than anything it will require people to learn new skills and change the way they have – or haven't – been doing things.

People are the core asset in publishing. If they don't have good ideas and get them down as quality content, all the technology in the world isn't worth a damn. At heart, publishing is a philosophy that sees content as its key asset. For starters, senior management must buy in and actively engage in the publishing process. If staff see that content publishing is something management expects everyone except themselves to do, then any publishing strategy will slowly and expensively run into the ground.

While senior management buy-in is an essential first step, the buy-in of all the knowledge workers in the organization is the next. People need to feel that the publishing strategy will improve their skills, make their workday more productive, and make them more money because it makes the organization more money. If staff members realize that their careers will progress the more quality content they create, it's surprising how enthusiastic they can become about creating content.

From an early stage, it's vital to isolate the important people who will be involved either directly or indirectly with the publication, and to get their buy-in and involvement. These people need to be fully engaged in helping define the reader, and the content for that reader. There's no point in deciding on a certain type of content, for example, if the people who are supposed to write it are either too busy with other jobs, don't have the required skills, or will resist because they were not asked for their opinion.

Equally important is to get buy-in and feedback from the reader. At every stage in the development and implementation of a publishing strategy the reader should be at the center. This means that there needs to be a constant exchange with readers to ensure that the right content is being developed for them, and that it is being presented in the right way.

If there is a golden rule for all publications it is to make sure that the person in charge understands publishing. The person (managing editor) running the website publication must have a real ability to understand the readers and what content they require. It helps too if this person can write.

Central messages that must be stressed again and again are:

- Publishing is about quality over quantity. It's about getting the right content to the right reader at the right time.
- Developing a publishing strategy is good for all of us. It addresses a core problem we all face – information overload.
- Publishing is not a threat but rather a huge opportunity for both the individual and organization.
- If you want to advance your career in an information economy, publishing skills are essential.
- Because knowledge is our key asset, we have no choice but to become better at getting our knowledge down as content. Publishing is how we do this.
- Quality content will be acknowledged and rewarded.
- The reader is king. You must write for the reader, not for your ego.
- The Web is a different publishing environment to other media. Therefore it requires a different approach.

Publishing strategy pitfalls

While traditional publishers understand the true value of content, many other organizations do not. Content is often seen as that thing you have to do after you've finished your "real" work.

People will derail your publishing strategy long before technology or any natural disaster will. While traditional publishers understand the true value of content, many other organizations do not. Content is often seen as that thing you have to do after you've finished your "real" work.

A great many people treat content with little more than contempt. They will rush off a few hundred words only under duress. They don't see the point. Then there are those who understand the value of content to such a degree that you can't stop them. They never pass up the opportunity to say in 5,000 words what can easily be said in 500.

Getting those who have the knowledge to write it down well is no easy task. If an organization does not have a culture that respects quality content, developing a successful publishing strategy will be a slow and perilous journey.

Technology can be depended upon to let you down. Much content management software has a snake-oil element to it. There are promises of "dynamic content," "personalized content," "automatic classification." It all sounds wonderful. You just have to buy this software, run your old content through it and instantly it becomes dynamic, personalized and automatically classified. Much of the promise is hot air.

The dark secret of publishing is that it's very labor-intensive. It takes real skills and real people to create, edit and publish quality content. Content is like computer code; it follows the classic rule of "garbage in, garbage out." If the content starts off as garbage, then running it through complex software will just turn it into dynamic, personalized garbage.

Many people have been burned by false expectations about how easy it would be to get others reading the intranet, extranet or Internet website. There is a perverse rule of publishing – while it can take years to make someone a loyal reader of a publication, you can turn them off with a couple of bad issues.

Publishing is no quick fix. It requires a slow, deliberate and consistent strategy. Publishing needs to be taken very seriously if it is to have any chance of success. However, when you consider that publishing is about putting the organization's most critical assets – its knowledge assets – to best use, that's not all that much to ask, really.

THE FIVE-STAGE PUBLISHING STRATEGY APPROACH

The five stages involved in developing a publishing strategy are:

1 Situation analysis.

2 Publication scope definition.

3 Information architecture design.

4 Building the publishing team.

5 Publishing technology design.

By and large this is a sequential process, although some of the activities in respective steps will overlap, and can be carried out concurrently. Not every publishing environment will require the same level of detail as we will now outline. However, as a manager or implementer of a publishing project you will have a checklist to work against.

This book has already covered all these areas in great detail. Here we will demonstrate a logical process for publishing strategy development and highlight key issues to be considered along the way.

Stage 1: situation analysis

Traditional in all planning and strategy development is a situation analysis. From a publishing perspective the following need to be covered:

- Organization website analysis.
- Industry and competitor analysis.
- Reader survey.

An analysis of the current website (if there is one) is required to establish how well publishing activities are being carried out. Questions that must be asked include:

- What set of readers is the current content targeted at?
- What type and quality of content is on the website?
- How are the content creation, editing and publication processes working?
- How well is content being classified? What about other metadata, search, navigation, layout and design?
- What sort of subscription, online community services are available?
- What's the state of the publishing organization?
- What sort of technology is being used to publish the website?

A similar analysis should be made of key competitor websites. With regard to the larger industry environment, important trends and best practice should be isolated.

Reader feedback should be sought at every stage of the process. At this stage it can involve a formal questionnaire or a meeting over coffee with a number of potential readers. There are key questions that need to be asked:

- What sort of content does the reader really need?
- In what format do they best like it published?
- How quickly would they like it published?

The results of the situation analysis should be properly documented and should become a reference point for the rest of the strategy development. It's essential that all parties involved in the strategy development have read and understood the results of the situation analysis. They will be particularly important with regard to defining the publication scope and designing the information architecture.

Stage 2: publication scope definition

First, get the reader right. Second, get the content right. After that it's about figuring out how the content will be created, edited and published. Dealing with these issues really defines the core publishing strategy. It will also become clear whether there is in fact a business case – whether the cost of doing it well is simply greater than the benefits that will accrue.

It may be that the initial ambition of the publication will have to be scaled back to something more realistic and feasible. Such critical decisions need to be taken during this stage. If not, then a lot of wasted time and effort will be put into further stages. It's a bit like designing a 100,000-seat stadium when the largest crowd will be 20,000. The small crowd will make the large edifice look like a joke. Alternatively, if you design a 20,000-seat stadium and 100,000 turn up…

Defining the publication scope requires realism. People get carried away when they start talking about what content they would like on the website. They rarely realize the cost and effort required in getting quality content published consistently. What people understand even less is that the launch of a website publication is really the beginning, not the end of the exercise. Who is going to write new content every day? Who is going to edit it? Who is going to publish the website?

As with every other stage it's important to establish measurables for what is agreed. There's no point in agreeing that the homepage will be updated at 10am every day, if there is no way of measuring that this in fact does happen. There's no point in agreeing a particular style and tone if the implementation of that style and tone cannot be measured. Too often content is treated as a fuzzy, almost artistic endeavor. If content is indeed critical to the success of the organization then it is critical that the performance of the publication be properly measured.

The important measurables to capture in the publication scope include the following:

- The reader – how many of them are required for success? Are they finding the content they need quickly? Are they coming back?
- Content – is the content being delivered to plan? Is it of the required quality? Is the cost of the content staying within budget?

Define the reader and content

Before any publishing strategy is developed, most people will have some idea as to who the reader is. However, at this point a concrete definition of the reader must be agreed.

The principal issue in defining the reader is one of value. Which reader given the right content can deliver the most value to the organization? There will be lots of potential reader types but probably only a few that are of real importance. The publication should target these.

A publication cannot be all things to all readers. Nor can it be all things to a specific type of reader. Again, be realistic. If getting the right content to the sales reps can significantly add value, then target them.

Quality content is expensive. While it will be important to brainstorm here, it's vital to quickly separate the essential content from the merely desirable. Defining the content requires decisions on the following areas:

- Agreeing on the key messages that the content must communicate.
- Isolating the essential content. Once this is isolated a calendar of events must be designed that will manage the creation and acquisition of this content.
- Deciding on delivery media other than the Web (email, mobile, etc.).
- Deciding how often the publication will be updated.
- Deciding language issues (for example, American English versus British English).
- Deciding the content forms (audio, video, etc.).
- Exploring at a high level the metadata required (classification, document templates, etc.).

It's important to spend adequate time defining the reader and content properly, as this will have huge implications for everything else that follows. Remember, getting the reader and content right is half the battle. Get it wrong and the game might as well be over – bar the shouting and the wasted time and money.

Design the create process

The create process involves:

- the actual creation of content on a day-to-day basis;
- how authors will be motivated and rewarded;
- the commissioning of content by editors;
- acquisition of content from third parties;
- content created by readers.

Factors that need to be addressed here include:

- the gap, if any, between the organization's current ability to create content and the content required;
- how this gap is going to be filled – through training or hiring;
- style and tone, word and phrase glossaries;
- policies on copyright, libel and other legal issues.

If a publication project is late or ultimately fails, the reason is often because the right content is not being delivered on time. Because content has for so long been treated as a commodity within organizations, there is a mistaken expectation that it can be churned out almost at will by staff. The truth is usually the opposite. Countless Web projects have been delayed because the content was not delivered on time, and when it was delivered it was not up to scratch.

Do not underestimate the difficulty in creating quality content on a regular basis. If necessary, go back and redefine the content required rather than plan for content that staff will simply not deliver to the required quality and publication schedule.

Countless Web projects have been delayed because the content was not delivered on time, and when it was delivered it was not up to scratch.

Design the editing processes

Content editing involves getting the content ready for publication. It covers the following:

- the contribution of content to assigned editors;
- the actual editing of the content;
- reviewing and correcting content that has already been published.

If the organization wants to publish quality content it must have a quality editing process. There is no way around it. Because of information overload, metadata should be an essential attribute of all Web content. It is recommended that the writer/author be responsible for completing the metadata for a particular document.

The essential importance of quality metadata can't be over-emphasized. If the metadata is poor, the reader will have difficulty finding the content they need. If they can't find it, they can't read it, and the whole expensive process is totally wasted.

Design the publication approach

Publication is all about presenting content to the reader in the best possible manner. Issues to be addressed include:

- the actual layout of the publication. (This will be more fully defined in the next section);
- whether such additional publication approaches such as subscription-based publishing should be used;
- what the reader interaction policy is;
- agreeing on content promotion strategies.

Don't expect that when you launch a publication readers will come rushing to it. Even if it's an intranet, an active promotion approach will be required to let the target readers know why they should visit.

The publication scope is the publishing strategy

Once you have defined the publication scope you have essentially defined the publishing strategy. The rest of the stages are really about planning for the implementation of this strategy. Therefore, it's important to properly document the publication scope stage, and that the results are presented to senior management before any further work is undertaken.

This allows management to review the detailed publication scope and to decide if this in fact is what was envisioned at the beginning of the process. At this point, certain modifications to the scope may be made before other stages are initiated.

No further work should be initiated until the buy-in and sign-off from the appropriate managers have been received for the publishing strategy as outlined within the publication scope document. A key decision at this stage will be whether there is indeed a business case for the proposed project. In any presentation, a cost-benefit analysis should be presented.

Stage 3: information architecture design

Information architecture is the structure that is used to publish the content in the most effective manner. Small websites don't have to worry too much about information architecture, but for websites with large quantities of content, designing an effective information architecture is a complex undertaking.

The following are key issues to address when designing the information architecture:

- Make sure that the publication scope has been properly signed off.
- Agree on the correct metadata approach (classification, document templates).
- Properly map out the search, navigation, layout and design approach.
- Get readers to test the architecture as it evolves.

Key measurables.

- How readable is the content on the website?
- How quickly can a reader find a particular document by using search and navigation?
- How quickly do the Web pages download?
- How does the website perform in a variety of browser types and versions?
- Does the website meet basic accessibility standards?

Design metadata, navigation and search

Metadata is crucial to the success of a Web publication. In metadata design we're dealing with two key areas:

- classification
- document templates.

When designing the classification it's important to remember that:

- it should be designed fundamentally from the readers' point of view;
- the quicker the classification can be mocked up the better. Get readers' feedback on whether they understand the classification;
- classification and navigation are very much intertwined.

In designing the document templates the following key issues must be kept in mind:

- Gather the metadata that is essential but don't try to gather too much, as the contributors will stop filling it out.
- Don't have too many document templates as this is only confusing. Most content fits into a small number of document types.
- The metadata you collect in the document templates should feed directly into the type of search the reader can carry out.

Make sure that best practice is adhered to when developing the search process. Remember, search is a key activity for the reader, yet most search processes are very badly designed.

Navigation is how the content classification is presented on the website. In designing the navigation adhere to the 10 principles of navigation design:

1 Design for the reader.

2 Provide multiple navigation paths.

3 Let the reader know where they are.

4 Let the reader know where they've been.

5 Let the reader know where they are going.

6 Provide context.

7 Be consistent.

8 Be familiar.

9 Don't surprise or mislead the reader.

10 Provide the reader support and feedback.

The reader likes a variety of ways to navigate around the website. Where appropriate, design for the following navigation options:

- core navigation;
- global navigation;
- personalized navigation;
- e-commerce/shopping cart navigation;
- homepage navigation;
- feature navigation;
- related navigation.
- classification path navigation;
- progress chart navigation;
- language/geographic navigation;
- document navigation;
- URL navigation;
- drop-down navigation.

Design general architecture elements

Depending on the scope of the publication, a number of other elements may need to be designed, including the following:

- Multiple language publication – if the publication is to be published in different languages an approach must be agreed early on with regard to how this will be done.
- Content conversion – if substantial quantities of content need to be converted from other formats, an approach needs to be developed. (This is not optimal but is a fact of life, particularly for intranets.)
- E-commerce integration – if there is an e-commerce facility on the website, integration will be a key issue.

- Accessibility – the information architecture design should meet minimum accessibility standards. A policy document on accessibility must be agreed and implemented.

- Interactive content tools – these include contact and feedback facilities, mailing lists, discussion boards, chat and customer reviews. Best practice must be adhered to.

- Subscription-based publishing – if subscription services are required, then they should be designed using best practice approaches.

Develop layout and design approach

Web design should champion simplicity. At every point in Web page design the following question needs to be asked – does this design optimize the readability? Following Web design conventions is a sign of strong rather than weak design.

There is often a conflict between what works well on the Web from a design point of view and what the corporate design standards dictate. For example, the organization may use a particular font in print material. However, this font may not work well on the Web. When such conflicts arise it's important to remember why the publication is being created in the first place – to allow readers quickly to find the right content. Everything else should be subsidiary to this objective.

Stage 4: building the publishing team

Having decided on the publication scope and the information architecture design, a clear view should have emerged as to what needs to be done to run the publication. The next stage is to build the publishing team to do this. Key members of this team will ensure that the publication is developed within a reasonable timeframe.

Critical issues that need to be addressed here are:

- the publishing workflows required (create, edit, publish);
- the design of a clear organization chart with functions and responsibilities;
- the impact on the wider organization;
- training requirements.

The measurables for the publishing team include the following:

A remuneration structure should be designed which rewards staff on how well they perform.

- How quickly is the content being published?
- How are readers being interacted with?
- How well are writers writing?
- How well are editors editing?

A remuneration structure should be designed which rewards staff on how well they perform on the above measures.

Define publishing workflows

The publishing workflows are: Create, Commission, Acquire, Reader-create, Contribute, Edit, Review, Correct, Publish. The information required to design the publishing workflows is fed directly from the publication scope document. Defining a particular workflow requires that:

- each step in the workflow be precisely defined;
- any interaction the workflow has with external systems is defined;
- the length of time it takes on average to complete a particular workflow be measured;
- the skill requirement to carry out the workflow is measured;
- the workflow is tested with real content.

Build the publishing team

In building the publishing team to run the publication, keep the following in mind:

- An experienced managing editor should be in charge.
- Each publishing workflow should be aligned with a job function.
- The publication scope will be used to define the number of people required to manage the various workflows.
- Hiring may be required where gaps exist.
- Training may be required where skill gaps exist.

- A publishing team organization chart must be developed.
- The key roles required in a publishing organization will be some or all of the following: publisher, managing editor, editor, copyeditor, writer/author, contributor, moderator, information architect, HTML coder, graphic designer, systems administrator/junior programmer, usability expert and marketing executive.

Stage 5: publishing technology design

It is not the objective of this book to explore or compare the various content management, subscription-based publishing or Web-logging applications available. Rather, we will highlight here important issues that need to be considered when choosing software options. Keep in mind the following:

- The publishing workflows and the information architecture requirements, particularly around classification, navigation, search and personalization, will set the requirements for what the content management software is supposed to do.
- Customization of software should be avoided as it will generally add greatly to the time and cost involved in implementing the solution. It is often better to adapt the workflows or other elements than customize.
- If customization is required it should be highlighted as early as possible as it may demand substantial work.
- Integration requirements with other software need to be carefully defined.
- Security will be an issue in a number of areas:
  - Where contributors are accessing the content management software both internally and remotely (from home, hotels, etc.).
  - When subscriber information is being collected. It is vital that such information is properly protected. If it is stolen or exposed, it can be disastrous for the reputation of the publication.

- The important technology measurables will include the following:
  - Acceptable levels of downtime (how often the website is unavailable).
  - Speed at which pages are downloaded to the browser.
  - Number of concurrent readers the system can facilitate.

FIGURE 12.1

Five-stage publishing strategy design

Situation analysis	Publication scope	Information architecture	Publishing team	Publishing technology
Internal Industry Reader	Reader & Content Create Edit Publish	Metadata & Classification Search Navigation Layout & Design	Workflows Team development Training	Server & networks Content Management Personalization Logging

CONCLUSION

The preceding five-stage approach – situation analysis, publication scope, information architecture, publishing team, and publishing technology – is a solid framework with which to approach publishing strategy development. However, it should not be seen as a rigid sequential process.

An unforeseen impact in one stage may cause a revisit in another. For example, it may be found that an editing workflow, as defined in the publishing team stage, takes just too long to complete, thus forcing a review of the editing process as defined in the publication scope. Flexibility is therefore important.

Keep the following in mind when finalizing the publishing strategy:

■ The reader is paramount at every step in the process.

■ It is equally important that the publishing team is comfortable, as are those who are expected to contribute and/or originate content.

■ Costs must be carefully controlled. Content has to prove that it can deliver real benefit to the reader and organization.

■ A detailed implementation plan should be drawn up.

No organization should attempt to develop a website without having a well-articulated publishing strategy based on careful analyses of the publication scope, information architecture, the publishing team and publication technology. Where a website already exists but is not meeting the organization's goals, reassessing the publishing strategy should be the first step towards improving the website.

Publishing has been with us for hundreds of years. While the processes and skills may need adaptation within a commercial Web environment, they provide a solid framework and way of thinking about content, its benefits and costs. It all begins with thinking of your website as a publication and the person who visits it as a reader.

INDEX

websites
   cluttered websites 133, 179
   of competitors 83
   multiple websites 75
   number of websites visited by readers 49
"where you are going" features 149–51
"where you have been" features 148–9
word and phrase glossaries 92
workflows 228, 229
World Wide Web *see* Internet; websites
writers *see* authors/writers

Xerox 51
XML (eXtensible Mark-up Language) 67–8, 130

Yahoo 13, 53, 136, 150, 160–1, 166
Yankee Group 94
"you are here" features 147–8

Zdnet.com 59
ZIP codes 155